RETURN OF THE
WOLF

by Steve Grooms

NORTHWORD
NORTHWORD PRESS
Minnetonka, Minnesota

NorthWord Press
5900 Green Oak Drive
Minnetonka, Minnesota 55343
1-800-328-3895

Cover design by Russell S. Kuepper
Book design by Kirstie Larsen

National Wildlife Federation® is the nation's largest conservation, education and advocacy organization. Since 1936, NWF has educated people from all walks of life to protect nature, wildlife and the world we all share.

For more information about National Wildlife Federation, write: National Wildlife Federation, 8925 Leesburg Pike, Vienna, Virginia 22184.

NWF's World Wide Web Site www.nwf.org provides instant computer access to information about National Wildlife Federation, conservation issues and ideas for getting involved in protecting our world.

©National Wildlife Federation, 1999 ™ and ® designate trademarks of National Wildlife Federation and are used, under license, by Creative Publishing international, Inc.

Library of Congress Cataloging-in-Publication Data
Grooms, Steve.
    Return of the wolf / Steve Grooms.
      p.   cm.
    ISBN 1-55971-717-3
    1. Wolves. 2. Wolves—United States I. Title.
QL737.C22G76 1999
599.773—dc21   99-14991

Printed in Malaysia

DEDICATION

This book is for Molly, my favorite daughter and wolf research librarian. Thanks for the help and never quit caring about wolves.

FOREWORD

Wolves spark intense emotions. Today they are revered as symbols of wilderness, worshiped as spirits of nature, and idolized as the ultimate social animal. Yet for some people, wolves still spark fear and hatred. While many people have neutral attitudes about most animals, people tend to have highly polarized attitudes about wolves.

That polarization makes it difficult to make rational, appropriate management decisions about wolves. That concerns me every day, because the mission of the International Wolf Center is to promote scientifically accurate information about wolves in order to help people understand, live with, and manage wolves in sensible ways.

Books like *Return of the Wolf* help that process enormously. In this book, author Steve Grooms provides a balanced, fact-based account of the relationship of humans and wolves. It is a remarkable story that is well told. He tells that story by describing wolves and wolf society, then by discussing several ongoing management controversies around North America.

Throughout the book, Grooms describes the great gap between wolves and the way people perceive them. Through it all, his own sense of wonderment about wolves and concern for them is apparent. This book promotes acceptance of wolves as they really are, without pretending they never cause problems for humans—yet it still argues passionately that wolves deserve to be part of America's natural world.

The wise management of wolves and other large predators will continue to be controversial, especially since so many people are removed from nature and must draw their information from books and media rather than direct experience. This book allows the reader to explore the evolution from concern over an endangered, misunderstood, and persecuted animal to the challenge of managing an intelligent predator that needs admiration and respect more than sympathy. Mastering this challenge is critical to the survival of the wolf and this book serves as a useful tool to that end.

Bill Route
Biologist, International Wolf Center

CONTENTS

Introduction

February is cold in the high Rockies, but wolves are well adapted for frigid weather. A solitary young male trots south through a mountain pass. His breath makes silvery vapor clouds that shimmer briefly in the moonlight. He notices nothing special as he passes out of British Columbia into the United States.

Where will he go?

If he turns east, he might enter Glacier Park. Glacier was empty of wolves for half a century, but today several packs exploit the park's generous population of mule deer. A new wolf arriving in Glacier might encounter aggression from the resident packs.

If he heads south and west, he might find his way to the Selway-Bitterroot, a large area of excellent wolf habitat in northern Idaho. The area already has some wolves, but there is room for many more. Yet if this young wolf were to stay in Idaho, he could get caught up in the bitter fight between wolf and antiwolf forces in the West. Doing so could cost him his life.

And if this young wolf were to keep trotting south and slightly east for several days, he might arrive at Yellowstone Park, that magic land of burping mud and faithful geysers. That wouldn't be far to go, not for a wolf. In Yellowstone, the young wolf would find more food than has been available to a wolf since rapacious settlers denuded the Great Plains of their fabulous wildlife abundance. He would also find himself in the symbolic center of the West's great wolf war. Incredibly enough, this wolf might ultimately be trapped and destroyed along with the other Yellowstone wolves because a judge has ruled the government's wolf restoration program violates the Endangered Species Act.

He, of course, knows nothing about all this. He is just a wolf. All he knows is that he is hungry and lonely. He is a predator with a hollow belly, a pack animal without a pack.

A small cloud drifts over the moon. The wolf flows along with the effortless, distance-eating gait of his kind. His long legs flash rhythmically, flicking mile after mile of landscape behind his plumed tail.

If the young wolf were to arrive at Yellowstone Park, he would become caught up in the West's bitter wolf wars.

He trots south, following ancient pathways used by wolves for centuries. His blocky feet make a putt-putt-putt noise in the crisp snow.

The wolves are returning.

They are coming home to lands where wolves lived since the glaciers left but where no wolves have been seen or heard for a long time—for years, for decades, for centuries.

Their return means different things to different people.

On an October night in the early 1990s, Kathe Grooms is driving north on Highway 13, headed for our family cabin along the shore of Lake Superior. Molly, our teenaged daughter, sits beside Kathe and chatters to keep her mom awake.

Near the mouth of the Brule River, the road bends east. Kathe's car takes the bend and is mounting a rise when two large animals appear in the headlights. They stop and swing majestic heads toward the approaching car.

"Deer, Molly! No. Are those . . . dogs?" Kathe knows there are no cabins nearby. It makes no sense that dogs would be out here at night.

For long moments, the animals do not move. In the Honda's headlights, their eyes glow with green fire like cyalume light sticks.

"WOLVES, Mom! They're WOLVES!"

The wolves are 30 feet from the car's bumper when they dive off the blacktop

and disappear in doghair aspen south of the road.

Molly has long adored wolves. Her room in our Minnesota home is virtually a shrine to wolves. Molly has gathered a serious library of wolf reference books, books her father would study in order to write this one. Wolf researcher Dave Mech is a personal hero of Molly's. Molly sleeps each night under the watchful gaze of 28 wolves in photos that hang on her walls.

Molly knows how special this moment is. At the time of this sighting, Wisconsin held only a few dozen wild wolves, and she has just seen two of them. Tears of joy well up in Molly's eyes.

Some of the wolves now repopulating former wolf country wear collars that beep locational signals to biologists. A few of those collars are state-of-the-art marvels that contain tiny electronic chips. Researchers with portable computers call out to the chips, asking what the wolf has been doing lately. Some wolves recolonizing empty habitat wear collars that speak to satellites orbiting above Earth's atmosphere. Is it just me, or is the idea of a wolf hooked to a satellite more than slightly strange?

Other wolves that are now returning to old wolf haunts wear only the classic badges of the hazardous life of a wolf—scars, torn ears, and bones that have fused together after being smashed in fights with prey animals.

A park ranger is doing a routine check of a campground in the Great Smoky Mountains National Park. She is puzzled by the sight of about 20 lawn chairs lined up in a row. The chairs are occupied by people clutching cameras. The ranger approaches a little girl with the group.

"What's goin' on, honey?"

"We're waiting for the wolf!"

"What wolf?"

"We put hot dogs on that rock over there. Now we're waiting for the wolf to come get them!"

Too late, an adult rushes over to silence the child. These people have camped in this spot for nearly two weeks. Seeing a friendly wolf, they decided to feed it. When the ranger informs them that they have compromised the wolf's future, they are deeply offended. They only meant to help.

The wolf is a highly endangered and rare red wolf. But now, because it is too tame to be allowed to roam wild, this wolf must be captured and returned to a zoo after just months of freedom.

Now and then, that wolf must dream of a magic land it once visited . . . a land

Wolves are returning home to lands where none have been seen for centuries.

without walls, a land where everything was wonderfully stinky and unpredictable, a land where hot dogs grew on rocks!

In some places, wolves are being restored to their former habitat with enormous effort and at considerable public expense. Dedicated professionals and ardent volunteers work together. The wolves arrive as confused travelers in kennels before being turned loose, their every movement monitored electronically by researchers.

In other places, wolves are restocking themselves, coming in on their own. Nobody invited them. Nobody helped them. They're simply doing what wolves have always done: strike out for new places to hunt, howl, mate, raise a family, and form a new pack of wolves.

A young black wolf strides across a gravel road as my car approaches. After stepping into the brush, the wolf turns to study me. I stop the car. Four feet separate the wolf's face and mine.

The wolf is coal black, with a white blaze on its chest. It stares at me with calm interest for several minutes. When I move the car to view his tail, only its eyes move.

"You're pretty damned cocky, aren't you?" I finally say. "You simply don't see me as any kind of threat."

For perhaps three minutes, the wolf's

Some wolves are restocking old habitat on their own. Nobody invited them. Nobody helped them.

hot golden eyes are locked on mine. It never blinks. Then it melts into the brush. In a lifetime among animals, I have never seen an animal so supremely comfortable with itself.

Months later, the encounter begins to haunt me. Another wolf has met another human and found him harmless, and that might not be good. Should I have fired my shotgun over its head to prove humans aren't to be trusted?

As part of the process of "delisting" the gray wolf in the western Great Lakes, the state of Minnesota holds a series of wolf management Roundtable discussions. What they reveal is the huge divide between different people's views of wolves.

At one meeting, an elderly couple testifies in tears. They live in a sizable northern Minnesota town where no wolf has been seen in this century. But a wolf has just killed their pet dog, right in their yard.

The old couple gets no sympathy from the woman representing an animal rights group. "You don't deserve to own a dog," she says. "You were irresponsible to leave a dog in a yard in wolf country."

Wolf country, in Minnesota, is now roughly the upper half the state, and expanding. Wolves live mere minutes north of the Twin Cities. In a matter of years, wolves might disperse into some suburbs. Food would be no problem. Deer are as common as minivans in many suburbs.

January 12, 1995. After twenty years of acrimonious struggle, the wolf has come back to Yellowstone Park. Hundreds of people cheer, hop, and howl as 14 wolves, encased in metal kennels, are driven through the great stone gate to the park. The celebrants include two heroes of the wolf restoration program, Hank Fischer and Renée Askins. This will be one of the happiest days of their lives.

Then the unthinkable happens. Just before the wolves are to be released, the Wyoming Farm Bureau gets a district court to issue a stay. The wolves cannot leave the pens for 48 hours while yet another legal fight is conducted. Television cameramen slip caps over their lenses, fidget, and wait.

Hours go by. These are wild wolves, and they are surely stressed by this unplanned-for confinement. In the afternoon, Interior Secretary Bruce Babbitt grimly notes, "If we don't get those wolves out soon, those cages may turn into coffins."

After a cruel day of waiting, the kennel doors are finally lifted. Moments

The wolf's hot, golden eyes remained locked on mine for perhaps three minutes.

later, the most famous wolves in the world step into the snow of Yellowstone, leaving the first wolf tracks seen there in nearly seven decades.

And all this time, wolves continue to come home, home to habitat where wolves flourished before being shot, trapped, snared, and poisoned. Many of them move at night, filtering through the underbrush unobserved.

It can be difficult. Some wolves reinhabiting old wolf haunts are whacked by the wheels of passing cars. Some breed successfully, then watch their pups sicken and slowly die of diseases against which evolution has given them no defenses. Some of the returning wolves are shot by people who mistake them for coyotes. Some are shot by people who hate government so much they mistake a wolf for all the outside forces threatening their way of life.

It is a sickening sound. The electronic monitor is blatting out a series of fast beeps that researchers call the "mortality signal." Wolf 532, a young male Mexican wolf, has not moved in four hours, which means he is almost surely dead. Trackers go looking for the wolf in the rugged mountains of eastern Arizona. Waving things that look like television antennas, they follow the beeps

to the gunshot corpse of 532.

In a matter of a few weeks, five wolves die by gunshot. A sixth is missing and presumed dead. Necropsies suggest that the wolves were shot by several different rifles.

What is going on here?

Wolf advocacy groups conclude there is a conspiracy by local ranchers, hunters, or both to throttle the Mexican wolf recovery plan before it can succeed. There are rumors ranchers were offering $10,000 to anyone who shoots a wolf. An animal rights worker claims to have taped a convict saying a rancher's group offered him a reward to kill the wolves. The report is denied. The front of the office of the animal rights group is shot up by someone in a moving vehicle.

One of the biologists in the program isn't so sure the killings were coordinated or planned. The wolves were shot during deer season, a time when a lot of people are traveling around the backcountry. In the words of a friend who manages nongame wildlife programs in the area, "This is a busy time, with hunters active, people out gathering firewood, and people coming up from the cities doing a little camping. Everyone has a rifle in the back window of the pickup. And the general practice is, you see a coyote, you shoot it." He mentions that Mexican wolves are not much larger than coyotes and are similarly colored.

A field biologist says, "What's so disappointing is that the wolves were doing well. They were leaving cattle alone and learning to hunt. Things were going so well."

But other wolves survive. And every year, there are a few more of them. And then a few more. Many people still shoot wolves when they see them, but not all people, and that thin ray of mercy is giving the wolves a chance to come back.

Yet people still have complicated, conflicting attitudes about animals. Wolves often pay a high price for that.

Federal trappers get the report a wolf has left Yellowstone Park and is apparently striking out for Canada, where she was born. She was the bravest and most beautiful of the wolves collected in British Columbia, the wolf that leaped at a helicopter with snapping jaws, trying to take it down.

Now she is traveling home with her pups. Because she wears a collar, she will be easy to find. When the mother kills some sheep, the trappers swoop in and surround the carcasses with traps. They don't want livestock depredations to inflame local antiwolf sentiment.

Since the wolf's radio signal indicates the wolves have moved on, the trappers decide they do not need to check their

A great mystery is why wolves, above all other large predators, have inspired so much human persecution.

traps every few hours as they should and ordinarily would have done. They do not know that a pup has split off the pack in order to feed on the sheep again. The young wolf puts a front paw on the pan of a trap set for its mother.

The trappers have been shadowed by an animal rights group that hates traps. They find the pup shortly after it is caught. They do not, however, phone authorities to report that a wolf pup has been caught. Instead, they camp on the site with cameras for about 36 hours, filming the pup's struggles. When the trappers finally collect the pup, the leg has had its supply of blood cut off too long. That leg must be amputated.

That wolf—perhaps the most beautiful wolf I have seen—now lives at the Wildlife Science Center, just north of the Twin Cities. The Center teaches young people about animals, especially wolves. Although the Yellowstone wolf cannot talk, he continues to teach youngsters complex lessons about people's attitudes toward animals.

For some people, the return of wolves brings humans a precious gift. It is the gift of a second chance. These people want to believe that our society is now a little wiser and kinder than our long, ugly history of wolf hatred would indicate.

For some people, the return of the wolves gives humans the gift of a second chance.

These people realize they risk disappointment by banking so many hopes on the return of the wolf. They know that things won't be perfect when the wolves come back. Somewhere, a wolf will slash through a bawling mass of sheep like a chain saw. Somewhere, an embittered man will shoot a wolf, attach its beeper collar to a log, and throw it in a fast-flowing river just to spite biologists.

Nevertheless, the return of the wolf seems a momentous turning point in history. Wolves are returning, and more people are welcoming them. Their return offers humans a chance to demonstrate new tolerance in dealing with North America's most fascinating and controversial predator.

Surely, things cannot go as badly as they did the first time around.

A young couple living in the wilderness of northeastern Minnesota is roused from bed one subzero winter night by an insistent knocking on the cabin window. Who could possibly be calling on them at this hour?

The knocker turns out to be a wolf with a radio collar and badly diseased lungs. After some initial alarm and confusion, the two people carry the wolf into their cabin and place him by the warmth of the wood stove. He does not struggle.

Throughout the night, the wolf accepts their care as if this kindness is what he expected, what he came for. But compassion and warmth are not enough to heal his lungs. In the profound darkness of predawn, his breathing grows labored until, just at sunrise, he dies in their arms.

CHAPTER 1

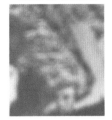

Wolves and Humans

The wolf was once a great ecological success story. Wolves hunted all of Eurasia and the New World, from sun-baked Mexico to the frozen Arctic. Wolves lived almost everywhere in the northern hemisphere, except the most arid deserts and the highest mountains. And wherever they lived, wolves were the top predator of large, hooved mammals.

Today, wolves all over the world have been eliminated from almost all of their original range. Some populations are hanging on in isolated remnant groups. Wolves have not been heard for centuries in many places where they once thrived. Perhaps no species has fallen so low in so many regions after succeeding in a diverse range of habitats.

The widespread collapse of wolf populations is all the more surprising when one considers the wolf's remarkable physical abilities and social structure. Most endangered species became endangered because they are too narrowly adapted or unable to respond to change. The wolf could not be more different. No hothouse flower, the wolf is one of the toughest, smartest, and most flexible species on earth. It should have been one of evolution's great winners, not a species flirting with extinction in so many regions of the world.

There is no dispute about how this improbable collapse happened. Wolves have declined through no weakness of their own, but because they have been subjected to centuries of ferocious persecution by humans. With the possible exception of the coyote, no other species has been singled out for such systematic extermination. In the late nineteenth century, a concerted effort was made to eradicate wolves as if they were a scourge that could not be tolerated at any level.

Of course, humans have persecuted other animal species also. Humans drove the bison to the brink of

Wolves once hunted all accross the New World, from Mexico to the frozen Arctic.

extinction, and people have traditionally killed venomous snakes on sight. Yet there is something uniquely nasty about the way humans have dealt with wolves. The wolf holds the wretched distinction of being the most misunderstood and persecuted animal in Western civilization. People have called wolves murderous, treacherous, gluttonous, savage, and cowardly. As if that weren't enough, wolves have been damned from church pulpits as sulphur-breathing minions of the powers of chaos and evil. Humans have hated wolves for centuries with a curious, hysterical energy.

Why?

WHO'S AFRAID OF THE BIG BAD WOLF?

It has become fashionable to blame wolf hatred on several European fairy tales. After all, it was a wolf that threatened to flatten the homes of three little pigs. It was a wolf that swallowed the silly duck in "Peter and the Wolf." Above all, in a tale some scholars believe represents male sexual aggression threatening feminine innocence, it was a wolf that gobbled Granny and seduced Little Red Riding Hood. Some historians believe that this last story alone provoked the deaths of millions of wolves.

But blaming old fairy tales doesn't explain much about our history of

It is too easy now to dismiss the fears people used to feel about wolves. They truly believed wolves would kill them if given any chance.

wolf hatred. It begs the question of why wolves and not other predators were singled out as symbols of evil. And it grants too much influence to a handful of fables. No, the true origins of wolf hatred lie elsewhere.

Obviously, wolves have suffered because people feared them. Very few northern hemisphere animals are capable of killing humans. While biologists tell us that wolves pose no significant threat to people, that's an extremely modern notion.

American settlers were less frightened by fairy tales than by all the presumably authentic stories they heard about wolves attacking people. For some reason, Russia and France exported more than their share of these tales. A typical example is the Robert Browning poem "Ivan Ivanovitch," in which a wolf pack pursues a sleigh across a wintry Russian landscape. To save their own lives, the occupants throw children to the wolves.

A gory variant of that story appeared in many newspapers just before World War I. This story described how "hundreds" of wolves devoured 118 out of a 120-member Russian wedding party. In a cowardly twist on the "women and children first" maxim, men from the wedding party pitched ladies and youngsters out of the sleighs. While the story seems comically macabre today, it was not questioned by readers in 1911.

Some bloody wolf stories had a basis in fact. The "Beasts of Gévaudan" were two animals that actually haunted a mountainous region of south-central France in the 1760s. The Beasts reportedly killed between 64 and 100 people before they were themselves destroyed. Because the Gévaudan animals were oddly colored and larger than normal wolves, modern researchers suspect they were wolf-dog hybrids. But such subtle distinctions were lost on people of the time.

Admirers of wolves today can't understand how people ever failed to appreciate the beauty of wolves. One answer lies in the way wolves were rendered by artists in earlier times. If an artist exaggerates certain features—the snout becomes longer and thinner, the teeth more prominent, the eyes narrower—a lovely animal appears menacing. If the wolf is also depicted as gaunt and desperately hungry, it becomes all the more threatening.

By contrast, contemporary Americans visualize wolves as they appear in photographs and paintings.

Overleaf: One reason the wolf-human relationship is so fascinating is that wolves apparently see humans as wolves, interpreting our behavior in their own terms.

The models for these newer works are captive or pet wolves that, while not quite chubby, are fed well and look it. The wolves we see in photos appear noble, friendly, and intelligent. They seem more like loving pets than slavering demons of the night. Most wild wolves I've seen are thinner and considerably spookier than the wolves of today's coffee-table books.

A friend who used to deliver mail around a wilderness lake using a dog team was chased for several miles by a pack of wolves. Even though Charlotte knew the wolves were probably responding to the fact that her lead bitch was in heat, she was unnerved by the chase. The next day, she bought a snowmobile. Snow machines can be quirky in cold weather, but they never attract wolves by going into estrus. Charlotte assured me that being chased by wolves is not fun.

All in all, it's too easy for contemporary Americans to belittle such fears. Terrified farm families living on the frontiers of civilization spent many sleepless nights while wolves moaned lugubriously from nearby forests. Those people not only "knew" that wolves killed humans but assumed that the animals would seize any chance to do so. They feared wolves in ways that are impossible for us to appreciate today and which we shouldn't dismiss smugly.

THE HOUND FROM HELL

The Christian religion has contributed to wolf hatred. The few references to wolves in the Bible are not complimentary. The central Biblical metaphor presents Jesus as the shepherd whose flock consists of his true believers. The image of Christians as sheep is not flattering, especially to anyone who knows sheep, but the real loser in this metaphor is the wolf. If Christians are sheep, wolves (since they prey on sheep) are murderers and possibly agents of the devil.

Wolves acquired all sorts of demonic significance in the tortured imaginations of medieval Europeans. Priests began preaching that wolves were Satan's minions. A fifteenth-century council of theologians studied the best research on the topic and proclaimed that werewolves undoubtedly existed. As a consequence, several men were burned at the stake or buried alive after confessing to murders they committed while they believed they were werewolves. A young man named Jean Grenier made a similar confession, but his death sentence was commuted. Grenier spent the last years of

his life in a friary, running around on all fours, eating rotten meat, and believing himself to be a wolf. It was so common for demented people to believe they were wolves that a name, lycanthropy, was coined to identify the malady.

Wolves somehow became associated with all the carnal appetites the church wanted to discipline and suppress. Incongruously, wolves—which are lucky indeed if they experience sex once a year—were depicted as symbols of promiscuity.

THE BEAST OF WASTE AND DESOLATION

When European settlers began to carve enclaves of civilization into the wilderness of North America, wolves became symbols of chaos and economic waste. Puritan preachers exhorted their flocks to make a "fruitful field" out of the "howling wilderness." The howl of the wilderness was supplied, of course, by

Some historians believe that the story of Little Red Riding Hood caused the deaths of millions of wolves.

wolves. Wolves were associated with all the godless wastelands that had yet to be tamed and converted to economic productivity.

The Europeans who settled North America assumed that mankind should hold dominion over animals. Animals were seen as valuable to the extent that they served man's needs. From such a utilitarian perspective, wolves were worse than useless. They not only lacked intrinsic economic value, they destroyed valuable livestock and wildlife. To this day, wolf researchers are dismayed by the taunt of wolf haters: "What good is a wolf?"

Both wolves and Native Americans were reviled as impediments to Manifest Destiny, the inevitable expansion of civilization from the Atlantic to the Pacific. Even those nineteenth-century Americans who admired Indians and wolves assumed they had to be eliminated because nothing could be allowed to stand in the way of the march of "progress."

When much of the West became sectioned off into livestock ranches, wolf hatred reached heights that seem barbaric even in the context of an already-bloody relationship.

Cattlemen laced carrion with ground glass and left it for the wolves. Trapped wolves were released with their jaws wired shut, so they would die slowly. Wolves were set

Large ungulates, like the fallen mule deer shown here, are the wolf's natural prey.

ablaze, much as "werewolves" had been burned at the stake in the Middle Ages.

Livestock interests kept pressing for more antipredator programs to make the West safe for cattle and sheep. All levels of government supported the effort to eradicate wolves.

The growing popularity of sport hunting provided another rationale for destroying wolves. Hunters believed that wolves were devouring precious populations of game animals. Killing wolves was an appealing form of game management, because it promised to create abundant game populations without requiring humans to restrain their own harvest.

One of the most enthusiastic wolf control agents in the 1930s was a young biologist named Aldo Leopold. Leopold believed that eliminating wolves would not only protect livestock but restore depleted stocks of elk, deer, and other game animals in the West.

AT THE TOP OF THE FOOD CHAIN

While it is simple to demonstrate that "Little Red Riding Hood" does not depict wolves accurately, debunking fairy tales distracts us from a more basic and potent motivation for wolf hatred: competition. Humans hate wolves because wolves compete with us for food.

We know that large ungulates—hooved, deerlike animals—are the wolves' natural prey. Wild and domesticated ungulates also happen to be the food most prized by humans. Whenever wolves consume a moose, humans are apt to think, "Hey! That's one less for us!" Whenever wolves consume a calf or sheep, the rancher who feeds his family by selling livestock says, "Ouch! That's one less for us!"

This natural competition has resulted in a pattern seen over and over throughout history. First, humans wipe out or deplete the wild ungulates that are the wolves' natural food. Then they fill the empty habitat with domestic livestock. When wolves turn to the only remaining food source—domestic animals—people respond with deadly force.

Hank Fischer, one of the foremost figures in wolf restoration, has written about this. At a time when many ranches were losing a significant share of their herds to wolves each year, it made sense to hate wolves. The wolves had little choice about what to eat, since humans had removed most of their natural food. Ranchers losing stock to wolves weren't troubled by notions of ecological coherence, as that whole world view had not been imagined. Hating to lose stock to predators, they decided the West wasn't big enough for wolves and humans.

Wolves and humans are predators perched uncomfortably near each other at the top of the food chain. Actually, what we call the "food chain" is a pyramid, with a broad base of vegetation, a trim midsection composed of prey animals, and a very narrow peak composed of predators. It is one of the most basic axioms of biology that food pyramids cannot support many predators. A corollary of that axiom seems to be that predators don't happily share a prey base.

I earlier described wolves as the top predator of large mammals, but that isn't true. Humans are actually the top predators of large mammals, which means humans and wolves have been and continue to be direct competitors for a limited food supply.

WOLF HATRED
AS SELF-HATRED

Even after contemplating the many factors causing humans to fear and resent wolves, it's difficult to account for the virulence of wolf hatred. Ultimately, it seems that wolves have suffered because they remind us too much of ourselves. Wolves, after all,

are the most intelligent and social animal on the North American continent. They are like us in many ways.

This theme has been developed in convincing detail by the writer Barry Lopez. Through the centuries, Lopez argues, we have projected onto the wolf the qualities we most despise and fear in ourselves. Wolves have not simply been misperceived, but demonized and made scapegoats in an outburst of self-contempt. Repeatedly, the wolf we have persecuted is not the actual wolf that hunts and howls in lonely places, but a conceptual wolf that we have invented somewhere in the spooky nether regions of our own psyches.

THE NEW POSSIBILITY

Two or three decades ago, the story of humans and wolves would have ended on that lamentable note. But something has happened recently to alter the old relationship, something dramatically new and about as difficult to understand as wolf hatred.

No person influenced American attitudes toward wildlife more fundamentally than Aldo Leopold, so it's fitting that an incident in Leopold's life marks the start of a new perception of wolves. Leopold and some companions were riding in the White

Two or three decades ago, it seemed that the story of wolves and humans would end on a tragic note.

Mountains of New Mexico when they saw a female wolf swim a river. She was met by six large pups that wriggled joyously to celebrate her return. The men's response was as reflexive as swatting a mosquito: they blazed away with rifles, then examined the results of their shooting. A wounded pup dragged itself into the rocks, while its mother lay bleeding by the riverbank.

And something astonishing happened. Looking into the eyes of the dying she-wolf, Leopold's sense of triumph changed to remorse: *We reached the old wolf in time to watch a fierce green fire dying in her eyes. I realized then, and have known ever since, that there was something new to me in those eyes—something known only to her and to the mountain. I was young then, and full of trigger-itch; I thought that because fewer wolves meant more deer, that no wolves would mean hunters' paradise. But after seeing the green fire die, I sensed that neither the wolf nor the mountain would agree with such a view.*

In that remarkable moment, centuries of wolf hatred collided with the basic decency and growing ecological wisdom of a single man . . . and the great shift from wolf hatred to wolf admiration became possible. It wouldn't happen soon—not even for Leopold, who continued to advocate wolf control for some time—but a new understanding of wolves was now possible.

Adolph Murie established himself as the pioneer of modern wolf research when he undertook his classic study of wolves in Alaska's Mount McKinley Park (now Denali Park) during the early 1940s. Murie had enough professionalism and honesty to see wolves as they were, not as he had been told they were. He described wolves as affectionate, cooperative animals that live in ecological balance with game populations. But few people were paying attention, and the old attitudes carried on.

A new climate of ecological awareness was being born three decades later when researcher L. David Mech published his book, *The Wolf*, in 1970. Mech wrote at a time when bounties had just been removed from wolves in Minnesota. The general public ignored wolves, while hunters, game managers, and farmers opposed them. Although *The Wolf* seems primarily addressed to scholars and students of wolves, the book became a crossover hit that sold to the increasing legions of wolf fans. Mech, an energetic and multitalented man, continues to pursue his favorite topic as a researcher, writer, manager, and photographer. More than any single person, he is responsible for creating a more tolerant public perception of wolves.

Shortly after Mech's book appeared, the U.S. Congress passed the Endangered Species Act of 1973. Wolves were among the first animals listed as endangered. That status brought wolves into the public eye and endowed them with a certain tragic, romantic identity they had never before enjoyed. Federal policy took a remarkable about-face. Government wildlife managers began plotting the restoration of wolves in regions where governmental programs had only recently succeeded in eliminating them.

It's impossible to document the impact of the countless wolf films that have aired on television in recent years. Beyond question, they have been potent agents for changing the public perception of wolves. Before Murie, virtually no human had actually seen wolves without looking through distorting veils of fear and myth. Now, that experience is routinely available to anyone with a television.

In just a decade and a half, the wolf has gone from scapegoat to object of adoration. Wolves have become the ultimate symbol of wilderness and of man's inhumanity to animals. Artists who once made a living cranking out waterfowl paintings now frequent zoo wolf exhibits so they can paint the

Today, wolves have become the ultimate symbol of wilderness.

animal that now dominates the wildlife art market. The Minnesota town of Ely, notorious in the 1970s as a bastion of wolf hatred, scrapped vigorously in the 1980s for the privilege of hosting the International Wolf Center. Mail-order catalogs can sell any product imaginable so long as it carries the image of a wolf. Americans are falling in love with wolves.

Library bookshelves now groan under the weight of all the revisionist, pro-wolf juvenile fiction. In *The True Story of the Three Little Pigs*, the author ("A. Wolf") protests, "Hey, I was framed!" Children are still aware of the Little Red Riding Hood legend,

yet they're more likely to identify with *Julie of the Wolves*. In that popular book, a little girl rejected by humans is befriended by wolves. Many youngsters now have a positive image of wolves.

Such a large change . . . and in just a decade or two! How could this have happened? According to one juvenile literature librarian, today's children are pro-wolf because today's books "present the scientific perspective on wolves."

Really? Are we witnessing the triumph of science over ignorance?

I don't think so. Consider Farley Mowat's *Never Cry Wolf*. Originally a

There are now three wolves keeping company with one another in the American mind.

book, it became a hit movie that lives on in television re-runs and video rentals. By presenting wolves as admirable and humans as vicious, *Never Cry Wolf* did for wolves what the movie *Dances With Wolves* later did for Indians: it turned an old stereotype on its head.

Never Cry Wolf must have presented unusual conflicts for wolf biologists like Mech. The book was a work of fiction that the author presented as nonfiction. In the act of rejecting pernicious old myths, Mowat created pernicious new ones. For example, wolves cannot live on a diet of mice, no matter what wolf admirers might prefer to believe. A few scientists were disturbed because they believed Mowat plagiarized some of his material. Yet in spite of its flaws and distortions, *Never Cry Wolf* was attractively written and sympathetic to wolves at a time when wolves badly needed friends.

Can a bad book be a good thing?

THE THREE WOLVES

The strange, anguished relationship between humans and wolves has thus taken another odd turn.

There are now three different wolves keeping uneasy company with one another in the American mind. The old demonic wolf lives on, especially in the minds of older, rural Americans. Their view is being refuted by rapidly growing numbers of wolf fans, many of whom adore wolves uncritically and regard them as inherently nobler than humans. Then there is the wolf of the biologist: a remarkable predator—neither demon nor saint—that has an odd ability to incite contentious management controversies. Unfortunately, the sober, factual image of the wolf is harder to promote than the other two.

Wolves were persecuted for centuries because they were reduced to symbols of evil. Now they are worshipped by people who reduce them to symbols of wilderness (once a negative value, now a positive one) and embodiments of man's many crimes against the natural world. People used to view wolves imperfectly through filters of greed and fear; they now view them imperfectly through filters of guilt and romance.

After all this time, it remains as difficult as ever to see wolves not as symbols, but as wolves.

CHAPTER 2

Wolves of North America

All carnivores evolved from an ancient group of meat-eaters called creodonts. These otterlike creatures gave rise to two new types of carnivores. One was a catlike group that lived mostly in dense forests and jungles, practicing an ambush style of predation. The other was a doglike group that moved onto the plains and evolved long, speedy limbs to run down prey.

In time, that second group produced the highly successful family of Canidae, the doglike animals. It consists of several genera, the most prominent being the genus Canis. Included in the genus are the gray wolf, *Canis lupus*, the red wolf, *Canis rufus*, the domestic dog, *Canis familiaris*, the coyote, *Canis latrans*, several jackals, and Ruppell's fox.

THE WOLVES OF PREHISTORY

Scientists have reconstructed the history of wolf evolution primarily through the painstaking process of analyzing fossil evidence. Conclusions first suggested by reading fossil evidence are now being confirmed or corrected by sophisticated analyses of genetic material. Those two sources of information recently allowed prominent wolf taxonomist Ron Nowak to propose a fascinating account of how wolves developed.

According to Nowak, coyotes evolved from foxes some four or five million years ago. Between one and two million years ago, the coyote line split into two groups. One group consisted of a slightly huskier version of today's coyote. The other group had more massive skulls and other lupine features. This new group, in fact, closely resembled today's red wolf. These wolfish coyotes underwent many changes in the Pleistocene, the most turbulent and intriguing evolutionary epoch.

In the Pleistocene, the only constant factor was change. Ice caps

Wolves may have evolved from coyotes between one and two million years ago.

formed, melted, and formed again. Seas rose and fell. Islands appeared and disappeared. From time to time, glaciers surged over the land like runaway bulldozers—scalping off old hills and throwing up new ones. Most significantly, the Bering land bridge appeared and disappeared, alternately connecting and isolating the American and Eurasian continents from each other.

Changing climates produced changing forage, which in turn fostered changes in the fauna. Glaciation and other events isolated animal populations for long enough periods to let them evolve uniquely. Then the reversal of those conditions set them free to move about again. In short, the Pleistocene was a sort of goofy laboratory in which evolution could run riot, experimenting with all possibilities and producing all manner of beasts.

And what beasts! They included giant condors, saber-toothed tigers, wild pigs big enough to carry teeth three feet long, and the aurochs, a highly belligerent bison that managed to survive into the seventeenth century. The Pleistocene also saw multiple tests of the "bigger is better"

The two skulls illustrate that a wolf is significantly larger than a coyote.

concept. This was a time of monster elk whose freakishly large antlers reached up to ten feet above the ground. The Pleistocene produced beavers as big as today's brown bears and bears twice the size of today's grizzly. Towering over them all was the mammoth, a shaggy sort of elephant that was as large as many of the great dinosaurs that had dominated the Jurassic period.

Wolves underwent many changes in this seething, complex time. The original wolves, smallish animals that hardly differed from coyotes, slipped across the Bering land bridge to invade Eurasia. They eventually landed in such places as Spain, Japan, and several countries of the Middle East. Some of those regions still contain populations of small, "primitive" wolves.

Meanwhile, in northern Eurasia, a cooling climate favored the development of a larger and more formidable wolf. This larger wolf eventually got the chance to return to the American continent. There it met at least two other wolves, the original coyotelike red wolf and an impressive animal called the "dire wolf." Dire wolves had massive skulls and prodigious teeth. Most dire wolves were significantly larger than today's wolves. Dire wolves apparently evolved their unique qualities in South America, later migrating back to North America.

Scientists believe the various types of wolf coexisted for some time because skulls of gray and dire wolves have been found together in California's La Brea tar pits. The dire wolf eventually disappeared, either because it didn't fare well in a time when prey animals were not so large, or possibly because early humans eliminated a predator that competed directly with them for favored prey.

Wolves underwent their most recent evolution in central Alaska, in a time when the region was a lush, green refuge surrounded by glaciers. Conditions favored the development of a larger gray wolf. Those wolves eventually spread out, invading western Canada, the Rocky Mountain area, and much of Siberia.

Thus the large gray wolves that developed in central Alaska are the most "modern" or recently evolved. Most wolf populations located far from Alaska represent smaller and earlier versions of the gray wolf, versions more like coyotes. The oldest and most primitive of all wolves is the red wolf of the southeastern U.S., an animal virtually identical to the very first wolf of all.

WOLVES AND DOGS

While some scientists believe dogs descended from wolves, others argue that the picture is much more complex. They believe that several different wolf-dog animals appeared at different times and different places in prehistory. These included a prehistoric dog something like today's mastiff, a wolfish canid, and an early type of hound. Today's wolves and today's many different dogs descended from these earlier animals, with a great deal of interbreeding taking place over hundreds of thousands of years.

In this view, while modern dogs and wolves share many qualities and behaviors, some dog breeds (sled dogs, collies, and shepherds) are much closer to wolves than others (hounds, terriers, and pugs). Many dogs exhibit such wolfish behaviors as caching food, howling at police sirens, and urinating on trees to mark their territories. Yet dogs of some breeds do none of these things.

In spite of these differences, which suggest a complicated evolutionary history, dogs and wolves have a great deal in common. The gestation period for both is 63 days. The most sophisticated genetic sampling techniques have never identified genetic markers that differentiate dogs from wolves.

But genetic similarity does not equate with social compatibility. Wolves, dogs, and coyotes frequently kill each other when they meet in the wild. That probably results from a basic, instinctive sense of competition. The more similar animals of different species are in size and form, the more directly they compete for the same food supply.

The different canids share more genetic compatibility than is common between different species. As one consequence, canids can and do interbreed to produce fertile offspring. The ability to interbreed is one definition of a "species," so in this sense dogs, coyotes, and wolves are a single species. That said, let's note that a Yorkie-poo trotting on a leash in a knitted sweater is a mighty long way evolved from a Yukon wolf whose face is smeared with gore to the ears from eating the steaming intestines of a moose it just killed. Some people continue to breed wolf-dog hybrids, ignoring the urgent advice of authorities who condemn this practice as irresponsible.

Canid interbreeding can bedevil managers trying to restore wolf populations. The most tragic example was the hybridization between coyotes and red wolves that almost destroyed the red wolf as a species. Managers

Wolves and dogs are identical in several biological respects.

trying to restore gray wolves must maintain careful records of wolf sightings as one index of how well the wolves are doing. But "wolves" seen by the public sometimes turn out to be wolf-dog hybrids, which is frustrating to scientists.

WOLVES AND THEIR PREY

Wolves evolved to prey upon ungulates, a term referring to all the large, hoofed mammals. Important wild ungulates include deer, elk, moose, sheep, and bison. Those are difficult animals to hunt. Most are hard to catch, and some are dangerous when attacked. Wolves could never prey efficiently on ungulates had they not learned to hunt cooperatively in groups.

This innovation—hunting in packs—is probably the most significant aspect of the wolf as a predator. Solitary predators are obliged to prey on animals their own size or smaller. But by hunting cooperatively, a pack of small predators can catch and kill large prey. Wolves kill adult moose, even though one moose weighs as much as ten or eleven wolves. To put that in perspective, consider the African lion. Although nine times the size of wolves, lions rarely pursue prey as large as moose. Wolves could not have emerged as the world's most effective hunter of ungulates had they not developed the ability to hunt in packs.

When wolves attack a moose, each wolf is attacking an animal ten times its own size.

Large ungulates are the natural prey of wolves. Since few other predators can take large ungulates, one might argue that wolves evolved their pack hunting style in order to take advantage of an abundant food source that was not being exploited. It can just as logically be argued that wolves prey on large ungulates because no other prey animals are large and abundant enough to reward the hunting efforts of a whole pack. This is a chicken-and-egg debate that chases its own tail; the point is that large ungulates are the logical prey for wolf packs.

Both wolves and their prey underwent millennia of evolutionary refinement in a process that biologists have likened to an arms race. When evolution produced a new and improved antelope—for example, a swifter model—only the quickest wolves could catch it. Because only the speediest wolves then lived long enough to reproduce, their genes brought about new and improved versions of wolves. The idea is neatly expressed in a Robinson Jeffers poem:

What but the wolf's tooth
whittled so fine
The fleet limbs of the antelope?

THE TWO WOLVES

North America contains two basic wolves, the gray wolf and the red wolf.

The animal most Americans mean when they say "wolf" is the gray wolf. The gray wolf was once widespread and common in North America. In fact, it originally occurred all over the Northern Hemisphere, from the latitude of Mexico City and north almost to the North Pole, except where the red wolf predominated in the southeast.

Taxonomist E. A. Goldman argued that 24 subtypes of gray wolves once roamed North America. But Goldman proposed that highly fragmented breakdown at a time when taxonomic "splitters" were dominant. "Lumpers" have prevailed recently, arguing that the similarities among gray wolf subspecies are far more important than the differences. Instead of referring to "the eastern timber wolf" or the "rocky mountain wolf" as if they were distinctive animals, today's scientists often talk about the "gray wolf of the Great Lakes" and "gray wolf of the Rockies." The gray wolf that today chases deer in Minnesota is essentially identical to the extinct "buffalo wolf" of the Great Plains and the extirpated wolf that once killed great stags in Scotland.

The animal most Americans mean when they say "wolf" is the gray wolf.

One reason for emphasizing the commonality of gray wolf subspecies is the way wolf-hating groups have twisted the Endangered Species Act to block wolf restoration by arguing scientists were restoring the "wrong wolf." With the exception of the Mexican wolf, which is genetically unique, biologists find much more in common among gray wolf subspecies than differences.

The red wolf, *Canis rufus*, is a special case. If it is a wolf, it is a distinct species rather than a subspecies of the gray wolf. Taxonomists continue to debate the legitimacy of the red wolf's standing as a species. Some argue that there are coyote alleles in the red wolf's genetic makeup, so maybe it is a sort of hybrid. In a recent development, some scientists think the red wolf is virtually identical to the wolf found today in Ontario's Algonquin Park. Others regard the red wolf as a version of the original wolf, some ancient ur-wolf from which all of today's gray wolves derived.

Biologists will probably never uncover enough reliable information about the original ranges of the two North American wolves, because wolves were often extirpated before

The original range of the wolf in North America is shown on the left; the current range on the right.

scientists could make careful observations. Serious scholarship on wolves began only about half a century ago.

In broad terms, though, the story of the range of North America's wolves is simple enough.

The red wolf is believed to have originally occurred in certain regions of the American Southeast, from coastal Georgia and Florida as far west as Texas. It might have lived as far north as the Carolinas and southern Illinois. If the Algonquin and red wolf are the same, this animal's range was probably much broader than scientists have thought.

The gray wolf was far more widespread. It originally lived almost everywhere on the North American continent, except for a patch of the Southeast that more or less corresponds to the range of the red wolf. Gray wolves occurred as far south as Mexico City, although not in the land adjacent to either coast of Mexico, or in the Baja or Pacific coasts of California.

FIVE ARENAS

In many ways, the most important distinction between different wolves today is not anatomical but political.

Wolves seem doomed to be controversial everywhere they and humans share the same space.

In the political sense, then, America has five arenas in which wolf management is hotly debated.

The first gray wolf endangered species recovery plan was developed for the western Great Lakes. This plan has been so successful it seems about to put itself out of existence. That is, wolves are just about to lose their official endangered status in the Upper Midwest. That will mark one of the most remarkable accomplishments in the history of wildlife management.

A different recovery plan brought about the reintroduction of wolves into central Idaho and Yellowstone Park. Wolves trapped in Canada were transported to empty wolf habitat where wolves could be expected to thrive. The plan has been ferociously fought all the way. This controversy has developed into one of those unique watershed management disputes that have great symbolic and historic importance.

A third recovery plan attempted to restore the highly endangered Mexican wolf to the wild, specifically into an area of extreme eastern Arizona. As this book goes to press, the Mexican wolf program is in tragic

tatters. When five of the wolves reintroduced to the wild were shot, the few survivors were whisked up and restored to the safety of pens. The program will go on, but is obviously in deep trouble.

A separate recovery plan exists to restore the red wolf in limited areas of the American Southeast. This program, now several years old, pioneered techniques that are being implemented in gray wolf restoration programs.

Alaska is an unusual case. No recovery plan exists for Alaska's wolves because they have not been extirpated or even diminished to "threatened" status. In fact, Alaska's wolves seem to be flourishing. Yet Alaska's wolf management has been extremely controversial.

Well, no surprise there. The wolf is the most controversial animal in North America. Where wolves don't exist, people fight about plans to restore them; where they do exist, people fight about plans to manage them.

The debate rages on today.

Alaska's wolves have long been the center of bitter management disputes.

CHAPTER 3

Meet the Gray Wolf

The "gray wolf" actually occurs in several colors, and the pelage of most wolves contains several shades of different colors. Gray wolves range from creamy white all the way to inky black. Pups from a single litter often show color variety, and wolf packs frequently include animals of different colors.

Like many fish, wolves are dark above and light below. A typical gray wolf has cream or white legs and tan sides. The long black guard hairs on the back and shoulders give wolves dark backs. The complex light and dark shading on a wolf's face dramatizes its expressions, which is useful for such highly social animals.

In effect, wolves wear two coats. The downy, highly insulating undercoat is so thick that a pointed finger can't penetrate through it to the skin beneath. When we look at a wolf, though, we mostly see the long, glossy guard hairs of the overcoat. Wolf fur has the unusual quality of not accumulating ice when struck with warm,

moist breath.

The wolf's majestic head frames a pair of eyes that photograph as amber but can seem to change. Lois Crisler, who lived with several semi-tame wolves in Alaska, described wolf eyes as "level and large and as clear as pure water, gray or gold or green according to mood and individual wolf." People who find themselves the subject of a wolf's stare are often moved to awe by the sense of power and intelligence it conveys.

Of all dog breeds, the malamute most closely resembles the wolf. Comparing a wolf to a malamute can show us how wolves differ from dogs. For starters, the wolf's brain is 30 percent larger. The wolf's head is significantly wider than the dog's head. That effect is accentuated by the "ruff"— those long, downward-slanting hairs that flank the wolf's face and give it a striking profile. The wolf's snout is longer and thinner, possibly because humans have bred dogs to look less threatening. A wolf's chest is narrow-

Gray wolves come in several colors, and most wolves in fact have several different colors in their pelage. The pure white Arctic wolf is an exception.

er and deeper, and a wolf is much leggier than a malamute of the same size. The lanky legs of the wolf terminate in feet twice as big as those of a comparably sized dog. (A wolf paw is slightly larger than an average man's fist.) Wolves hold their tails many ways, but never in the characteristic manner of many dogs, curled up over the back.

Gray wolves are adapted for living in cold climates. When a wolf wraps itself in a ball and tucks its nose in the insulating muff of its tail, it can sleep in minus 50-degree weather. A wolf's massive feet help it move on snow. Because of its narrow chest, the front legs are mounted close together. This arrangement enables wolves to run efficiently, laying down tracks in a single neat line. These are useful adaptations for an animal that must often break a path through snow.

A wolf makes its living with a set of 42 teeth. The most impressive are the four large canine teeth. The big canines are over an inch long. Their primary purpose is to pierce the hair

The ancient Greeks believed a wolf's gaze could strike a person dumb.

and hide of such shaggy brutes as moose, so the wolf can gain a secure hold. The molars at the back of the jaw have the power to crunch huge moose, elk, and bison leg bones. Between the molars and canines are the carnassial teeth, which shear skin, sinew, and muscle.

Gray wolves are smaller than most people think. Most weigh between 50 and 100 pounds, females about 20 percent smaller than males. Size is related to geography. The wolves of some desert regions may not exceed 45 pounds, and the Mexican wolf is small enough to be mistaken for a coyote. Weights of 115 pounds are not uncommon in cold regions. The largest wolves come from Alaska, the Yukon, some areas of Canada, and the former Soviet Union. Those regions occasionally produce individuals weighing 175 pounds. Dave Mech mentions an unconfirmed report of a Yukon wolf weighing 227 pounds. That animal would have created a stir if it had strolled through a sixteenth-century French village!

In length, male wolves approximate the height of most humans: they are from five to six-and-a-half feet long (nose to tail tip). Of that length, about 18 inches is tail. Male wolves usually stand 26 to 32 inches at the shoulder, so an average human could stand with a leg on either side of a wolf at the shoulders.

THE WOLF'S SENSES

Biologists don't know a great deal about the sensory capabilities of wolves. Serious wolf study began only a few decades ago, and there have been more urgent questions to answer than how well a wolf can see or hear.

While a blind wolf wouldn't live long, scientists consider vision the wolf's least developed sense. Vision primarily becomes important to wolves during chases when the prey is near. Wolves can apparently detect moving objects at distances where they cannot discern stationary objects. They see very well at night, and that's important. Especially in areas where they're heavily hunted, wolves do much of their traveling and hunting in the dark.

A wolf's sense of hearing is at least as acute as a human's and probably much more so. A wolf's concave external ear funnels sound vibrations to the inner ear much like a human hand cupped behind an ear to detect faint sounds. Wolves can hear howls as far as six miles away, possibly ten miles away in open terrain. They can also discriminate between tones that are very similar.

Biologists claim that wolves are a

hundred times better at sensing odors than humans, and some say a million times better. Researchers have seen wolves scenting prey a mile and a half away, although that would require a favorable wind. Scent surely plays a larger role in a wolf's life than scientists have documented, since even highly trained biologists cannot detect the odors that might be influencing the wolf behavior they observe. We can usually only infer the role of scent since we cannot perceive the odors directly.

Wolves are highly intelligent. I'm not aware of any empirical studies measuring wolf intelligence, but there is abundant anecdotal evidence. A retired wolf trapper once claimed that wolves would occasionally hit one of his snares but escape by dodging back quickly. When that happened, said the trapper, he could forget about putting out any snare sets for that wolf . . . or any wolf in that pack. After one wolf learned about snares, the entire pack would become wary of snares.

Some captive wolves learn to escape from their pens, after which they are almost impossible to confine in any enclosure. These Houdinis do not escape through random effort, but by using remarkable problem-solving powers. Wolves have remembered former human masters after a separation of three years.

Wolves seem especially adept at learning by observation. Some learn to open doors with their mouths after watching people using doorknobs. A research assistant once created a machine that would dispense a treat when its treadle was pressed. He demonstrated this machine to a penned wolf. When he attempted to teach the machine to a second wolf, he was dumbfounded to discover that this wolf already understood the whole business. The second wolf had observed the earlier demonstration from its enclosure.

Because wolves live in groups, all pack members can benefit from the experience of one wolf. The ability to learn by observation must have benefited wolves enormously over the centuries.

WOLF CAPABILITIES

The mobility of wolves is legendary. According to a Russian proverb, "The wolf is fed by his feet." On the tundra, where prey animals are separated by great distances, wolves may travel 40 miles a day to feed. A wolf usually trots along at five to nine miles per hour, maintaining that pace for hours. Pressed by hunters, a pack in Finland

moved 124 miles in a single day. Packs have traveled 45 miles in a day even with no pursuit. A wolf is generally on the move eight hours a day, so wolves spend a third of their lives (about half of their waking hours) trotting or running. It's unlikely that any human athlete, even a world-class marathon runner, could match the aerobic conditioning of the average wolf.

When attacking, wolves can turn on a burst of speed of up to 35 miles per hour. They explode toward their prey in bounds that cover as much as 16 feet. Wolves can maintain a hot chase speed of 25 miles per hour for up to 20 minutes, although most chases are either abandoned or concluded with a kill much sooner than that.

Wolves exert a bite-pressure of 1,500 pounds per square inch—twice the crunch of a German shepherd. Wolves can crush bison thighbones three inches thick and smash moose skulls in their jaws. A human armed with a sledgehammer would need several blows to equal those feats.

Wolves are extremely hardy. They

Wolves can smell objects buried beneath deep snow.

survive injuries that would kill animals with softer constitutions. Half the wolves autopsied in an Alaskan study had suffered at least one major injury, such as a broken rib, leg, or fractured skull. A broken rib or leg means something different to a wolf than to a dog. No veterinarian is available to treat a busted-up wolf, and the wolf clings to life by being a capable hunting athlete. The kind of nagging injury that would put an NFL wide receiver out for four games might be fatal to a wolf.

The most aggressive wolves in a pack, the ones that initiate attacks on large prey animals, are particularly liable to be injured. The skeleton of one alpha male showed several healed injuries from earlier prey encounters, including several broken ribs (possibly from different encounters), a kicked-out tooth, and a fractured jaw. That wolf was finally killed when a deer drove a hoof through its skull.

A wolf in Minnesota lived for several years on three legs. When researchers caught her, one of her back legs was broken and swinging uselessly. A veterinarian removed the bad leg, after which the wolf was released. She not only survived with just one back leg, but went on to make history as one of the principles in the most unusual romantic triangle

in wolf research literature. The three-legged female slipped away and had a two-hour "date" with the alpha male of an adjoining pack. To complicate things, her alpha male apparently mated with another female in his pack. Such sexual shenanigans, while common among humans, are a rarity among wolves.

I photographed that wolf recently. She might make history again by becoming the longest-lived wolf on record.

THE VITAL WOLF

All the individual senses and abilities of wolves are remarkable enough, yet we underestimate wolves when we examine them piece by piece. The wolf is greater than the sum of its parts. Science hasn't yet found a way to measure the wolf's tenacity and its ferocious will to live.

Wolves lead extremely strenuous lives, often while carrying heavy loads of internal and external parasites. Researchers never touch wolf scat with a bare hand, because of all the parasite eggs likely to be present. Wolves are also capable of fending off a wide range of canine diseases that regularly kill unvaccinated dogs. Wolves have survived gunshots and major injuries that, by any reasonable calculation, should have been fatal.

As Russians say it, "The wolf is fed by his feet."

ARE WOLVES
A THREAT TO HUMANS?

Years ago wolf biologists—reacting against centuries of hysterical wolf hatred—spread the word that wolves do not attack humans. That was basically true then and remains essentially true today.

Wolf fans have reduced that statement to the comforting notion that wolves "never have and never will" attack humans. This position is popular with children and wolf romanticists. Unfortunately, it continues to be spread by some wolf advocacy groups, although more careful biologists and advocacy groups have changed their message to one that is slightly more cautionary. In response to the "never have and never will" refrain, a biologist recently told me he thought wolves "probably did, haven't lately, but might again."

For a while, wolf biologists endorsed an accurate and scientifically defensible statement that was reassuring. But every time there was an incident, they had to tweak the message. When captive wolves in an exhibit killed a worker, it was necessary to add that *wild* wolves hadn't killed a human. That statement now would claim (and I'll italicize the qualifiers): "There is no *confirmed* record of *an unprovoked, non-rabid, non-hybrid, wild* wolf in *North America seriously* injuring a person."

That's seven qualifiers. The statement now sounds like a weasel-word disclaimer written by a corporate attorney.

This is getting silly. The reason it is getting silly is that people who love wolves are hung up on the idea that they "never" have attacked a person. Why people cling to that idea so tenaciously is a matter for psychologists to explain. It is time for people who admire wolves to talk more sensibly.

It wouldn't hurt to add wolves to the list of animals that very rarely attack people, but that have and might again. That list would include cougars, black bears, and grizzly bears. The list would also include such animals as rattlesnakes, bison, sharks, bees, coyotes, white-tailed deer, moose, and scorpions. "Man's best friend," the dog, kills a dozen or two of us each year!

Consider the black bear. In spite of their great strength, bears are so timid that a child can send most bears fleeing by banging a pot. Yet a few unlucky people meet an aggressive bear that is having a bad day, and not all live to tell the tale. It would be foolish to say black bears "never have

Although wolves are hardy, mortality rates among pups are normally high. Only the most fit survive.

and never will" attack humans, although they very rarely do. (And when they do, often some human stupidity is involved.) Similarly, it is not responsible to insist that wolves would never attack humans, as if they were born with some saintly code of honor unique in the animal kingdom.

We need to be careful when interpreting wolf-human interactions. In 1996, in Ontario's Algonquin Provincial Park, a wolf grabbed an 11-year-old boy by the face and tried to drag him out of his sleeping bag. The wound required 80 stitches. It isn't clear what this wolf intended. This semi-tame wolf often played with campers, running away with tennis shoes and other gear. It might have been trying to get at the sleeping bag.

Another Algonquin wolf, a "super-tame" animal that had been photographed almost every day of the summer of 1998, made two attacks on children that have to be considered close calls. In one case, an alert father stood between the wolf and his four-year-old daughter. The wolf kept feinting and trying to get at the child. Two days later the same wolf grabbed an infant and threw it a short distance before being driven away. This unnaturally bold wolf had probably been getting food from tourists.

In view of several concerning incidents with super-tame wolves, Algonquin park officials are considering new management protocols.

Once tolerated because they were thought harmless, exceptionally tame wolves might now be removed as a precaution. As one official put it, "I'd rather remove a wolf before than after it attacks a child."

Why haven't wolves attacked people in the past? They've certainly had no end of opportunities and abundant provocation (think of all the snoopy biologists shinnying down dens to count pups). Now wolves are dispersing into settled regions of the western Great Lakes, and people are forever pressing into wolf country to hike, hunt, and fish. The potential for wolf/human contacts has never been so great, and yet people move safely in wolf country.

Two facts probably explain why wolves generally don't attack people.

First, wolves have learned from bitter experience that humans are the most deadly animal on earth. For centuries, people have killed wolves at virtually every opportunity. Most wolves flee when they see a human.

Second, people don't present the cues that trigger wolves to attack ungulates. An upright human looks, smells, and moves nothing like a deer (and in fact might resemble an angry bear). Wolf attacks are usually triggered by the flight of a prey animal, especially if that animal does not move with the fluid grace of a healthy individual. Animals that stand their ground are usually not attacked, and humans usually stand their ground.

Yet some people who know and like wolves believe they might attack under certain circumstances.

Gray wolves recently killed or maimed about 74 children in India. These kills, documented by scientists, involved wolves that had lost their fear of people and were stressed by an absence of wild prey. Apparently a small group of wolves decided children were prey animals.

In 1998, a man I know was camping in Minnesota's Boundary Waters Canoe Area Wilderness. Three wolves came into his camp and were so unafraid that the camper almost had to kick them away. They came back a second time and were again reluctant to leave. That night the wolves returned and stole food five feet from the tent where several humans were asleep. These wolves did nothing aggressive, yet they seemed to have no fear at all of people. Examples of such unnatural boldness are becoming more common in the Midwest.

Some wolf authorities now believe that decades of federal protection might have produced a new wolf, what might be called the "post-persecution wolf." Wolves are highly intelligent. It would be remarkable if

they did not sense that people are no longer a serious threat to them. This doesn't mean they will begin attacking people, yet one of the two factors preventing wolves from attacking people—their great fear of humans—is fading for the wolves in some areas.

We should respect but not fear wolves. If a wolf does attack a human in the future, it will almost surely be a "tame" wolf, one that has been emboldened by interacting with people and getting food from them. And it will almost surely attack a small child, not an adult. Wolf experts now tell mothers they should not leave a small child unattended in wolf country. It's just common sense.

Because "tame" or habituated wolves are so much more dangerous than people-fearing wolves, we owe it to wolves to keep them afraid of us. It is bad for people and bad for wolves to

let wolves become too comfortable around humans. We should never confuse wolves with pets. They are wild animals, not dogs—and dogs kill people every year. We certainly should never feed wolves to make them like us. Almost inevitably, that will cost the wolf its life.

The basic message is the same. It is essentially true that wolves don't attack people. But they are powerful predators that should always be viewed as being potentially dangerous, just like other large predators. As long as we keep wolves wild and follow common sense precautions, wolves do not pose a significant threat to humans. Humans and wolves can live together, although it is not clear we can do so peaceably with absolutely no management policies to keep wolves wild and in places where man-wolf conflicts are unlikely to happen.

While wolves generally don't attack people, they should be respected in the way we respect other large predators.

CHAPTER 4

Wolf Society

Wolf experts flinch when they hear someone say, "Wolves always . . ." or "Wolves never . . . ." While wolves are orderly creatures that behave according to certain basic principles, they're also flexible and difficult to predict. Wolves are social animals. Much of a wolf's personality and behavior is learned, not genetically fixed as "instinct." This makes wolves less stereotyped in their behavior than many animals. It also makes them fascinating.

THE WOLF PERSONALITY

Generalizing about the "wolf personality" is tricky for several reasons. It is difficult to say which personality characteristics are inherent and which are acquired through learning. Wolves have been described as extremely "shy" and fearful of humans. But that shyness might have been a natural response to centuries of persecution, which suggests the fear that was learned could now be unlearned as wolves live near humans without experiencing aggression from

them. Wolves are becoming increasingly bold in the Western Great Lakes states where laws and community standards have reduced the rate of persecution.

Second, social animals like wolves don't all have the same personality. That only makes sense. After all, dogs—even dogs from the same litter—exhibit wonderfully diverse personalities. Inuit and other native groups have occasionally been amused to discover that a visiting biologist thought all wolves were alike. They aren't.

Third, a wolf's personality changes as the wolf matures and assumes different roles within the pack. Pack leaders are decisive, outgoing, and self-confident. Pack underlings are obsequious and loyal to the leader. Some low-ranking adults are playful and goofy, blending aspects of the adult personality with puppy qualities. But when a low-ranking wolf assumes alpha status, it acquires some version of the classic alpha personality.

The wolf's society is not always a polite one.

With all those qualifications, what can we say about the wolf personality? The key to understanding wolves is to understand the social dynamics of the pack.

For the pack to adhere and function, its members must live cooperatively. A wolf pack is held together by bonds of affection. Adolph Murie wrote, "The strongest impression remaining with me after watching the wolves on numerous occasions was their friendliness." Reunions between pack members are celebrated with a display of joy that has been called the "jubilation of wolves." Anyone who has owned a dog can understand the bonds of loyalty that link pack members. The affection that pack members have for each other is the same "love" that dogs extend to their human families.

Pack members cooperate extensively with each other. Wolves cooperate when hunting, and they spend much of their lives hunting. Low-ranking members sometimes perform "baby-sitting" chores, and all pack members may feed the pups. At times, pack members have nurtured injured wolves. In Alaska, a wolf caught in a trap was apparently fed for days by other pack members. However, in the same circumstances, trapped wolves have been eaten by pack members.

Conflict within the pack is abnormal and deeply disturbing to wolves. That's hardly surprising, since social discord is incompatible with the efficient functioning of a pack. One of Lois Crisler's wolves was so distressed when it witnessed a dogfight that it separated the combatants, yanking one back by the tail. A good deal of snapping and snarling is common within packs, but serious aggression is not.

Wolves are so docile in certain situations that people have damned them as "cowardly." For example, most wolves caught in leg-hold traps are oddly compliant. A trapper interviewed by Barry Lopez described approaching a wolf in one of his sets. The wolf whined softly and extended the trapped foot, as if requesting help. A retired Minnesota wolf trapper told me, "I never saw a wolf I couldn't trust." By this he meant that trapped wolves accept their doom with dignified composure. "They weren't cowards," he explained. "They just knew they'd had it."

What accounts for this timidity in an animal powerful enough to easily kill a human? Researchers speculate that because wolves live in hierarchies, they naturally defer to self-confident humans as they would to an alpha wolf. This tendency of wolves to "read" humans as if they were

wolves is one of the many ways the relationship of humans and wolves is curious and deep.

The readiness of wolves to view humans as wolves shows up frequently in wolf literature. Lois Crisler and her husband found that they could communicate with their wolves by adopting wolf body gestures. Lori Schmidt, who maintained a pack of captive wolves for the International Wolf Center, learned to anticipate which sorts of people would provoke her wolves. "Flaky" people and people with low self-esteem, she says, upset the IWC wolves. R. D. Lawrence was told by a person who often took a leashed wolf into schools that the wolf would occasionally growl quietly at a child. Invariably, said the keeper, the teacher would later identify the child as an outcast who was rejected by other children.

A biologist told me about one of these "ambassador wolves" that was so friendly to children it was taken into classrooms to educate youngsters about wolves. Then one day the handler noted the wolf's attitude toward children had changed. It was pacing and looking at the children in a way that suggested it was measuring them for a meal. The wolf was quickly retired from its ambassadorial duties.

Each wolf knows exactly where it ranks in the pack's "pecking order."

Intriguingly, the handler thought the change began when the wolf witnessed a child throwing a temper tantrum, flailing at the floor with arms and legs. At the same time, the wolf met an autistic child. Something about those two children gave off the "I am out of control, I am prey" signals that wolves get from panicked sheep. This wolf never misbehaved, but its handler feared it had learned to see children as prey.

Wolves are not sloppy in their social relations. They live in a highly structured social system and take great pains not to upset the integrity of that system. Each wolf knows exactly where it ranks in the pack's pecking order and what actions, accordingly, it may and may not take.

Wolves are usually hostile toward wolves that don't belong to their own pack. Packs often kill lone wolves that trespass into their territory. Turf wars between packs sometimes break out along territorial borders. At other times, wolves can switch packs without suffering violence. It seems likely that packs are highly intolerant of outsiders when food is scarce and

Wolves don't live in perfect harmony. Small acts of aggression reinforce pack structure, and that helps packs avoid more significant aggression.

more relaxed when food is as abundant as it is in Yellowstone, for example. Genetic research is now showing that wolves from different packs will sometimes cooperate and mix peacefully when they have family ties.

While admirers of wolves are discomfited by the aggression wolves sometimes show other wolves, it is simply another aspect of pack social dynamics. Dave Mech has observed the normal way a wolf in the wild dies is by starvation or by being killed by other wolves. Alien packs and even unattached single wolves represent a threat to a resident pack, so they are often dealt with harshly. In this regard, as in others, wolf packs resemble human street gangs, offering their own members affection and support while exhibiting territorialism, violence, and intolerance toward outsiders.

The wolves' innate hostility to competitors may explain why they kill coyotes and dogs. Wolves raised with dogs are different; they view the dogs as fellow pack members. But wild wolves encountering a coyote or a dog will often attack it.

Unfortunately, some animal lovers who have had a beloved pet killed by wolves are now wolf enemies.

Wolves are usually hostile toward outsiders that don't belong in the pack.

THE PACK

A pack is basically an extended family of wolves. Most packs consist of a dominant breeding pair and any number of their offspring. Of course, it isn't quite that simple. Very little about wolves is! Some packs include "aunts and uncles." Occasionally a nonrelated wolf attaches to a pack. Now and then an alpha wolf lives long enough to be toppled from its throne by a more vigorous pack member. The old wolf remains a pack member, albeit with reduced status.

A wolf pack is not a loose collection of animals, but a tightly knit, organized group. Pack members stay together much of the time, usually hunting and defending territory together.

Biologists use names for different classes of pack members. The cocky, happy leaders who do the breeding in a pack are the "alphas." Adults ranking below the alphas are the "betas" or "biders," so-called because they are biding their time, waiting to advance in rank. In large packs,

Above: A wolf pack is a tightly knit, organized group.
Right: The wolf is a social animal, and its great success derives directly from the benefits of the ways individual wolves cooperate and act for the common good.

some unfortunate animal may become the scapegoat or "omega" wolf that must tolerate abuse from all other pack members. The pups occupy a special position that is not, strictly speaking, above or below the omega wolves.

There are two lines of dominance, one male and one female. The alpha male enforces the male dominance line and the alpha female enforces the female line. The alpha female is particularly aggressive in defending her exclusive right to breed. Among wolves (including red wolves), there are several documented cases of mothers killing daughters in fights over access to the breeding male.

Wolves engage in many small acts of dominance that reinforce the clarity of the pecking order. Dominant wolves pick on lower animals at odd moments, for no apparent reason except to demonstrate that they have the right to do so. Many of these tests come at eating time. While the seemingly gratuitous displays of superiority look nasty to humans, they prevent more dangerous conflicts that could result from ambiguity about status. Few people who believe that wolves are morally superior to humans would

enjoy life as a low-ranking member of a wolf pack.

Researchers no longer claim that packs are always led by males, or even that a pack typically has a single leader. In many situations, such as choosing a route or deciding to attack a prey animal, one wolf clearly leads. Most observers have assumed that this is the alpha male. But at times, the alpha female dominates the male, so leadership is shared. Packs usually respect the wishes of leaders, although Dave Mech once observed a leader abandon a plan that was unpopular with the pack.

Packs can number as few as 2 wolves or as many as 30. Most packs in the continental U.S. number between 5 and 10. In Alaska and northern Canada, packs frequently number between 10 and 20. A pack in Glacier Park recently included 20 animals—unusually large for the continental U.S. The group eventually split into two packs that were unusually tolerant of each other, visiting each other's territory without conflict.

A pack changes size throughout the year. It achieves maximum size in late fall, when a fresh cohort of pups joins the hunt. The pack dwindles to its nadir in early spring, when its numbers are depleted by winter mortality and the defection of young wolves that seek their fortunes apart from the pack. Wolf biologists working to meet recovery plan goals maintain separate counts on pups and adults; the pups die so often that many wolf population counts leave out the pups or list "wolf" and "pup" numbers separately.

Pack coherence is dynamic rather than static. Life in a pack offers individual wolves certain survival advantages, particularly when it comes to killing large prey animals. Wolves are strongly motivated to stay within their packs by those benefits plus the emotional "glue" that bonds pack members to each other. Yet all pack members below the alphas must sacrifice self-interest to live in the pack. They constantly defer to the alphas in such matters as breeding rights and access to food. To some extent, self-interest and group unity are in conflict; thus there are always centrifugal and centripetal forces acting on a pack. When the pack grows too large, stress sets in, the center no longer holds, and the pack splits.

Pack size seems related to prey size, although the connection is not a simple one. Wolves that prey on small animals typically live in very small groups. Wolves that prey mostly on deer usually form packs of 4 to

Dominant wolves may pick on other pack members for no apparent reason.

6 animals. Wolves preying on such formidable animals as moose typically include 14 or 16 members. Yet, after a pack numbers 5 or 6 adult wolves, adding members provides no hunting advantage . . . and that confuses the issue. The relationship between prey and pack size probably has less to do with killing than dining: large packs more efficiently consume large prey, and small packs more efficiently consume small prey.

COMMUNICATION

A social animal cannot afford fuzzy communications. For example, a wolf must be able to discriminate between a bluff and a genuine status challenge. While wolves cannot make speeches or send faxes, they make themselves understood quite clearly with a combination of vocalizations, body postures, and scents.

Wolves growl, squeal, bark, whine, and, of course, howl. Whimpering or whining conveys friendly intentions. Crisler was probably referring to whimpering when she described her wolves "talking." She wrote, "The wolf talking is deeply impressive, because the wolf is so emotionally stirred. His eyes are brilliant with feeling." Growling is a threatening noise. Barks signal alarm.

Wolf howls are one of the most moving and haunting sounds in nature. An old trapper described a pack howl as "a dozen train whistles braided together." The first time I heard wolves howl, I was camping in a canoe wilderness, sleeping in a nylon tent that suddenly seemed thin and insubstantial. Though I knew I was in no danger, that doleful moaning in the darkness made my hair stand up in places where I hadn't known I had hair.

Wolves throw themselves into howling with evident joy. Crisler compared howling to "a community sing." She wrote, "Wolves love a howl. When it is started, they instantly seek contact with one another, troop together, fur to fur. Some wolves . . . will run from any distance, panting and bright-eyed, to join in, uttering, as they near, fervent little wows, jaws wide, hardly able to wait to sing."

Each howling wolf sings a unique note. When Crisler howled with her wolves she learned that if she trespassed on the note a wolf was singing, it would instantly shift up or down by a note or two. "Wolves avoid unison singing," Crisler concluded. "They like chords." Possibly, but biologists believe the function of polyphonic singing is to increase vocal impact. Wolves singing two different notes produce three tones—the two being sung plus a harmonic. Fred Harrington, a researcher who did extensive work with howling, noted that an observer can distinguish between one and two howling wolves, but "any more than two sound like a dozen."

Ulysses S. Grant and his guide once heard a stirring chorus of wolf howls. The guide asked how many animals were making the sound.

Each howling wolf sings a unique note.

Grant foolishly decided to prove that he was no dude. Although he was certain that so much sound could only be produced by a huge pack, Grant said that just 20 wolves were howling. The men soon rode up upon the pack. Two wolves sat on their haunches, howling with open mouths held close together like barbershop quartet singers.

Howling celebrates and reinforces pack unity. In that regard, wolves resemble such human packs as street gangs and athletic teams, which have their own solidarity rituals. It is accurate—though a little fanciful—to translate some group howls as meaning something like: "We're the Mink Lake pack, and we're alright! Trespassers here are in for a fight!"

Like "aloha," the howl of a wolf has several meanings, and which one applies is determined by context. Wolves howl to reinforce territorial claims, particularly when challenged by the howls of an intruding pack. Fred Harrington concluded that wolves howl most readily when they have something to defend, such as pups in a den or a fresh kill. Pack members howl back and forth to keep track of each other when visual communication isn't possible. A howling session can reunite a pack that has

broken up to hunt within an area. Sometimes a pack howls after making a kill. This may be a device to keep alien packs away from the kill, or it might be the wolf equivalent of the "high fives"—jubilant gestures used by athletes following a big score.

Wolves respond to human howls. Researchers often howl to trigger a reply that confirms a pack's presence in a certain area. Wisconsin wolf biologist Adrian Wydeven monitored one remarkable old male wolf nicknamed "Whistler" for many years. During a fall howl census, Wydeven got a response from Whistler that sounded distinctively lonely. Although the pack had at least three pups in spring, by now there was just one adult. Weeks later, Wydeven howled at the same location, and was thrilled to hear a chorus from a whole pack. Although the impression might have been subjective, Whistler now sounded happier. Researchers John and Mary Theberge describe the distinctively "mournful" howl of wolves in a pack that has just lost a member to a violent death.

The willingness of wolves to howl back at people has created a curious sort of tourism. Many groups and agencies now sponsor howling trips to known pack locations. After all,

Before the pups can join the hunt but after they are weaned, they get food by nuzzling adults, who then disgorge food.

howling is about the only way in which a person who's fascinated by wolves can experience direct contact with a wild wolf. It's thrilling to howl into the darkness of a wilderness area and listen as a wolf answers you. Of course, the wolf may be saying something like, "Buzz off, dammit!" But it is talking to you, which is pretty exciting even if the conversation is rude.

Body language and facial gestures help wolves maintain the pecking order. The faces of most wolves are tinted in ways that highlight their changing expressions. Like mimes, wolves have plastic, variable faces that are marked to dramatize their changing emotions.

Various body postures allow wolves to convey messages. A wolf saying "hello" drops its head to the ground, exposing its vulnerable neck in a gesture of submission. Dominant wolves intimidate lesser pack members with fixed stares. In wolf society, making eye contact is aggressive posturing, not good manners. Wolves also express dominance by such gestures as standing up to ride across the back of another wolf.

A wolf's tail is the semaphore that signals its attitude. High tails indicate dominance and high spirits, although there are fine nuances of tail height and position that allow a wolf to communicate specific messages.

Submissive animals tuck their tails tightly under their bellies. Even untrained observers can spot dominant and submissive wolves by noting tail postures.

Scent is the wolves' third medium for social interchange. Scientists know less about scent because, unlike other forms of discourse, humans cannot perceive scent directly. Researchers can only infer its function by watching wolves respond to its presence.

Alpha males and females raise their legs to urinate, spraying scent up high where it will be conspicuous. Lesser pack members of both sexes squat like female dogs when urinating. Urine depositions mark the boundaries of a pack's territory. Like the spray-painted graffiti used by a street gang, these "Keep Out!" signs are particularly dense where territorial boundaries are close together.

Scent helps wolves navigate through their territories. Wolves leave scent-marks at significant points, such as trail junctions, creating olfactory points of reference.

Trappers used to believe that wolves moved around their territories

Wolves have "mental maps" that help them find their destination.

in rigid patterns; some thought they always moved clockwise, for example. Researchers now know that wolves retain superb mental maps that allow them to leave a familiar trail and bee-line cross-country to a particular destination.

Other uses of scent are more obscure. Wolves often defecate near such man-made objects as aluminum cans. Wolf trappers hated finding piles of dung beside their exquisitely disguised trap sets, because the wolves seem to be mocking their professional skills. A more plausible interpretation is that the dung simply marks a new or unique object that has appeared in their territory.

TERRITORY

Territorialism is not understood as well as some other aspects of wolf biology, mostly because it's difficult and expensive to study. Many research assistants must monitor many wolves wearing collars over long periods of time in order to learn where the wolves do and do not go. Some of this research is now being conducted using radio collars monitored by satellites, although neither collars nor satellites are cheap.

People often assume that wolf territories are as rigidly bordered as nation states. The image is misleading. Territories sometimes overlap. More often, adjacent territories are not

Wolves sometimes encroach on each other's territory, but doing so can be risky.

contiguous, like national borders, but are separated by "buffer zones."

Territorial borders also fluctuate, changing size as packs change size. There may even be a seasonal dimension to territories, meaning that habitat defended by a pack in February might not bear defending in June. Like so many aspects of wolf society, territories are subject to constant revision.

It's clear that wolves need a lot of living space. Whereas a deer might live in a territory of less than half a square mile, most wolf packs defend territories of 50 to 150 square miles.

The smallest area that can serve a pack in good deer country is 30 square miles, whereas packs in Arctic areas must hunt territories as large as 1,000 square miles.

Bob Cary, a long-time observer of wolves, describes wolf territories in northeastern Minnesota as "like Swiss cheese," with the holes representing established territories and the cheese signifying buffer zones. Prey animals concentrate in the buffer zones. Cary has learned that his chance of bagging a deer for his family improves if he hunts the cheese and avoids the holes.

CHAPTER 5

The Year of the Wolf

The wolf's year breaks down into two rather different halves. During most of the fall and winter, the pack lives on the run. In spring and summer, the pack has a more or less fixed address while it concentrates on raising a new generation of wolves.

The annual pattern described here applies to most—but not all—wolves. Some wolves that prey upon caribou, for example, have evolved a different lifestyle, following the great herds as they migrate.

THE PANTRY

The wolf's reproductive cycle is synchronized to take advantage of seasonal food abundance. Wolves prey primarily on ungulates. Deer and moose typically have a hard time in late winter. They enter the spring in poor condition, making them vulnerable to wolves at just the time when wolves need a reliable source of nutrition for their pups.

Denning wolves must do all of their hunting in a limited area, rather than roving widely as they do the rest of the year. Most ungulates give birth early in summer. Newborn moose, caribou, and deer are vulnerable to predation. Thus the wolves' pantry is restocked with a fresh bounty of young ungulates at the very moment the pack must confine its hunting to a limited area.

The bounty doesn't last. As wolves and other predators make repeated withdrawals from the supply of prey animals, finding food becomes more of a challenge. The pantry gets bare as the year progresses.

DISPERSERS

Now and then, a young wolf decides to strike off on its own. A bider, in other words, becomes a disperser. Most dispersers are yearlings, and both sexes disperse.

These defections from the pack are remarkable. Wolves are social animals, so a lone wolf is a wolf living in an atypical way. It must be difficult for the wolf to sever the emotional

The wolf's year breaks down into two distinct halves.

bonds that have held it within the pack. Some dispersers need to work up to the schism by undertaking a series of short experiments with independence.

Dispersing also exposes wolves to great hazards. Acquiring food is diffi-cult and dangerous even for a pack, so a lone wolf hunts at an enormous dis-advantage. Dispersers risk being attacked for trespassing on the terri-tories of other wolf packs. For all these reasons, mortality among dis-persers is high.

In the weeks before mating, breeding wolves begin to groom and fondle each other.

Why disperse, if doing so is risky and difficult? Some young wolves simply get fed up with low pack status. In particular, they may resent being denied the right to breed. Researchers think it's significant that dispersers often leave shortly before the mating season, a time of high tension within the pack. While it can be misleading to compare wolves to humans, one might compare a young pack wolf to a 20-year-old human still living at home. That young human might think, "Man, I gotta get out of here! Mom and Dad get all the best food, everyone picks on me, and they don't let me have sex!" And so it is with wolves.

No single pattern applies to all dispersers. Some remain within their former pack's territory. Others take off on a line, as if they had a compass, a map, and a distant destination in mind. Dispersers can move astonishing distances. One wolf traveled over 500 miles before finding what it was seeking. Other dispersers drift into the buffer zones between pack territories. Now and then, a dispersing wolf encounters a resident pack and becomes accepted as a member. In some such cases the visitor is accepted, possibly because it has blood ties to the new pack.

Dispersing wolves search for unoccupied territory and an unattached wolf of the opposite sex. Some succeed in both objectives, although many more do not. Researchers believe that such a happy meeting of two dispersers is the main way in which wolves form new packs.

The mechanism of dispersal ensures that wolves make the best use of their habitat. When conditions are favorable (when food is abundant), dispersers survive and form new packs; when conditions are unfavorable, dispersers die, decreasing the local wolf population. Dispersing also minimizes genetic problems that could arise from inbreeding.

COURTSHIP AND REPRODUCTION

Each year, a wolf pack must renew its claim on the future by offsetting attrition through reproduction. But since overpopulation is as threatening to wolves as inadequate fertility, several devices limit the animal's reproductive potential.

Wolves do not usually reach sexual maturity and reproduce until they are three, four, or five years old. Some wolves reproduce when they're two years old, and a few zoo wolves have done so when just a year old, but wild wolves generally reach sexually maturity later. Wolves apparently mature earlier when food is abundant, when the pack has suffered high mortality, or when abundant habitat makes dispersal and early breeding a workable strategy. The variable age of sexual maturity is one of the shock absorbers that keep wolf numbers aligned with the capacity of the territory to support them.

The main limitation on reproduction is social. The alpha male denies other males access to the breeding female, and she prevents other females from associating with the alpha male. As a result, most packs produce just a single litter.

Some packs include a second breeding female and thus a second

litter of pups. Pups from the second litter don't enjoy the same prospects as the alpha pair's pups, but if food is plentiful, many pups from the second litter may survive. Second litters are another way in which wolf numbers are adjusted in accordance with the food resources of their habitat.

In the weeks before mating, the breeding pair engages in a number of affectionate gestures, grooming and fondling each other. Less romantically, the breeding pair performs "RLUs" (raised leg urinations). When the female is in estrus, her urine is bloody. Researchers who monitor wolf populations look for double urine marks in the winter snow. The marks represent the promise that another litter of wolf pups will soon be nuzzling the mother's teats in a nearby den.

The mating season can be protracted over a period of weeks in late winter or spring. Northern wolves mate later than southern wolves, probably because northern ungulates produce their offspring later in the year. Breeding couples sometimes slip away from the pack to copulate in private. They aren't modest; they simply need to get away from pesky, nonbreeding wolves.

Very little about wolf biology is cut-and-dried. Sometimes the alpha male or alpha female does not choose to participate in breeding. Nobody knows why. Mated pairs are usually faithful to each other while both partners survive, but not always. As mentioned earlier, wolves have been known to conduct illicit affairs. Irregular sexual behavior might be more common than is now known, for few packs have been studied intensively enough to document deviances.

After breeding, the female seeks a den. Old den sites are often used year after year, and some have been used continuously for many decades. The den Murie observed in Alaska is still producing young wolves today, more than 50 years later. If a female cannot find a suitable den, she digs one. She might evict some smaller animal from

Wolf pups are winsome creatures that have melted the hearts of wolf trappers.

its home and enlarge the domicile to suit her needs, or she might settle for a depression in the ground.

Dens are usually caves, holes in the ground, or chambers formed by a jumble of large rocks. A den must be dry and secure, situated in good hunting territory, and located near water. Wolves seem to prefer den sites near high ground, so they can survey their surroundings. While lounging in elevated areas may help wolves spot approaching danger, researchers also believe that wolves simply prefer a scenic view while they're resting.

PUPS

Wolf pups are born 63 days after the breeding pair mates. Litters range in size from three to nine pups, but most consist of four to six. The pug-nosed pups are born blind, deaf, and capable of only a limited amount of scooting around in order to stay near the warmth of their mother. Pups weigh about a pound at birth but grow rapidly. Once they hit their growth stride, wolf pups can gain three pounds per week.

At several weeks of age, young wolves are so winsome that they have

Above: Wolf pups engage in all sorts of playing and fighting, which is actually purposeful since it polishes skills they will need as adults.
Right: When the pups are big enough, the pack moves to a rendezvous site, which is above ground and situated near good hunting areas.

been known to melt the hearts of men who make their livelihood by killing wolves. One wolfer wrote, "I have never had to do anything that goes against the grain more than to kill the pups at this stage. Potential murderers they may be, but at this time they are just plump, friendly little things that nuzzle you and whine little pleased whines."

At about three weeks, the pups begin venturing into the outside world. They romp at the den mouth and begin play-fighting. At this age, little wolves form bonds with the rest of the pack.

All pack members involve themselves with the wolf pups. Even the alpha male usually exhibits tolerance for their tomfoolery. In zoos, some unbred female wolves undergo the hormonal changes of pregnancy, in what is called a "pseudo pregnancy," later producing milk and nursing the pups. Wet-nursing has not been confirmed among wild wolves, but it may exist. Low-ranking pack members often become "aunts" and "uncles" with special bonds to the pups.

Wolves introduce pups to solid food in an ingenious way. Each day, pack members radiate out from the

At about three weeks, pups begin to explore the outside world.

den to hunt, while the mother remains behind to care for her offspring. Successful hunters fill up with meat, then return to the den, where they disgorge a meal for the pups and the nursing mother. The disgorged food provides the pups with tenderized, chopped-up meat that their digestive systems can handle. Later on, pack members bring undigested meat, like a deer haunch, to the pups.

Starting very early in life, little wolves engage in endless hours of roughhousing. All the pouncing, stalking, and fighting serves two critical functions. The pups are acquiring skills they will use to hunt real prey in a few months. At the same time, they're establishing their own dominance hierarchy.

When the pups reach about nine weeks of age, they're mobile enough to permit the pack to move to a "rendezvous site." Dave Mech describes these as "essentially a den above ground." Rendezvous sites are secure areas near water, where the pups can cavort in safety while the rest of the pack hunts. Some rendezvous sites are used year after year, like dens. If the pack makes a kill, the adults may move the pups to the kill site rather than the other way around—another way of creating a rendezvous site.

Sometime in early fall, the pack hits the trail again with the pups running along. Though the youngsters are now full-sized and look like adults, they can do little more than cheerlead during attacks on prey until they become a year old. The first year of life is a harsh form of schooling. Young wolves that fail to receive passing grades are not alive for long.

CHAPTER 6

Wolves and Their Prey

It seems so simple: Surround a deer, cut it down with a few bites, then *bon appetit!*

But for wolves, acquiring food is anything but easy. While animals that eat browse or grass can count on eating almost every day, wolves frequently go days between meals. Sometimes the fast stretches to weeks.

NO DAINTY EATER

Wolves do indeed "wolf" their food. Four wolves once consumed most of a mule deer in four hours. A wolf can bolt down a meal of 18 pounds of meat—the equivalent of a man devouring a 40-pound steak—at one sitting. Hungry wolves eat until their bellies are stretched to the limit, lie down to digest for several hours, then get up and do it all over again. Old-time wolf hunters knew it was relatively easy to sneak up on logy, "meat-drunk" wolves.

The wolf's digestive system is adapted for processing food quickly. Because its metabolism runs at such a hot pace, a wolf must drink copious amounts of water to avoid uremic poisoning. That's one reason den sites and wolf travelways are usually near water.

Wolves consume as much of their prey as they can immediately after the kill. They usually leave behind only a few scraps of hide, the skull, and perhaps the stomach contents. After a kill, the pack either camps at the site or revisits the carcass until even the bony lower legs have been eaten. When a pack abandons a kill, almost nothing remains to indicate that an animal weighing as much as 1,000 pounds was consumed at a site. When wolves attack livestock like sheep, they can consume so much of the victim that hours later the only evidence is a bit of pink wool blowing about. There might not be enough evidence of a wolf kill to warrant compensating the rancher who suffered the loss.

In the process of devouring their prey, wolves swallow large amounts of bone and hair. Veterinarians tell dog

The most dramatic moment in the hunt occurs when prey and predator make eye contact.

owners to never feed bones to their pets because sharp bones can puncture soft stomach or intestinal walls. But in a wolf's stomach, sharp objects are wrapped in hair until the package resembles a furry cocoon.

This explains the bizarre story about the wolf scat that contained a Mepps Spinner. The Mepps is a popular fishing lure that carries an unusually sharp treble hook. Because that fishing lure was encased in a mass of feltlike hair, it passed through the wolf without incident.

Okay, but how did a fishing lure get into a wolf? Researchers have a hunch. The wolf that excreted the spinner was a female with a den near a blue heron rookery. She frequently swung by the rookery to check under the trees for food. Perhaps a fish hit an angler's spinner and bit the line. Along came a heron to snatch this fish, struggling with a spinner in its gills. The heron might have served the fish to its young before kicking the bony head out of the nest. The wolf then ate the fish head, spinner and all.

WHAT THEY EAT

Wolves aren't fussy eaters, although they are definitely carnivorous. They'll consume almost any meat they can acquire, including birds, fish, hares, lizards, mice, and worms. The fact that wolves eat maggoty carrion suggests that their energy budget is too stringent to let them bypass an easy meal, even if that meal is spoiled. A common interest in carrion might explain the odd partnership that exists between wolves and ravens. Ravens follow wolves to feed on their kills. In fact, a good way to locate wolves is to look under a raven flock. Large ungulates are the most suitable prey for wolves. Depending on where they live, wolf packs mainly prey upon deer, moose, caribou, elk, sheep, bison, or musk oxen.

That doesn't mean small animals are unimportant to wolves. Beavers and hares can play a critical role by providing nutrition at a time of year when it is especially needed. Wolves rarely hunt prey smaller than beavers. Any mousing they engage in is casual, and might arise more from boredom than hunger.

PREDATOR-PREY RELATIONS

One of the most complicated and controversial aspects of wolf biology is the impact wolves have on prey species. Early research on this topic emphasized how difficult it is for wolves to catch healthy ungulates.

Later research has shown wolves to be adaptable predators that are capable of surviving even in difficult times. Research on predator-prey relations is greatly complicated by differences in geography, climate, the species compositions of the predator-prey systems, and whether humans are also part of the system.

In general, wolves cannot kill whenever they choose. They traverse large territories and hunt strenuously to find enough food to sustain themselves. It has to be that way. Any predator capable of killing at will would decimate its own food supply and quickly become a footnote in evolutionary history. For a predator-prey system to function over time, parity must exist between the eater and the eaten.

Wolves aren't fussy eaters.

And it does. Deer are usually too alert to be approached and too quick to be caught, once they bolt. Moose sometimes outrun wolves and sometimes fight them off with flailing hooves that strike like sledgehammers. Caribou, even the calves, can usually outrun wolves.

Yet wolves survive. One way they survive is by traveling mile after mile until they locate a vulnerable animal. This is why wolf territories are so large. Putting it the other way around, wolves wouldn't range so far if it were easy for them to kill the animals that live closer to them.

Prey animals become vulnerable in a number of ways. Some suffer from arthritis, disease, parasites, or injury. Some prey animals are unwary, slow, or indecisive when attacked. Very old and very young animals are especially vulnerable to predators. Sometimes a harsh winter will make whole groups of ungulates too weak to escape, and under these circumstances wolves may engage in "spree" killing. For example, if wolves discover a group of nearly starved deer trapped in a yard, they might kill all or most of them in one bloody binge. Given that much food, the wolves might then dine on choice parts, leaving the rest. This kind of feeding, while not typical, does occur.

All this does not mean that wolves cannot catch healthy animals. Sometimes they can, although the odds favor the prey unless it's weakened in some way. Wolves cannot afford to waste endless amounts of energy chasing healthy animals. They concentrate their efforts on individuals they're likely to catch.

Many animals killed by wolves would have died even if the wolves had not come along. When researchers examine wolf kills they find that a remarkably high percentage of the victims have skeletal deformities or injuries, which means that they were already in trouble when the wolves found them. By weeding out sick and parasitic animals, wolves might benefit healthy members of ungulate populations. By culling the stupid and slow animals from ungulate herds, wolves ensure that only the fittest live to pass on their genes.

This is summed up in the concept of the "balance of nature." The basic idea holds that predator species and prey species exist in equilibrium. Wolves control deer numbers by preying on the weakest individuals, and the deer control wolf numbers by being difficult to catch.

Yet things aren't nearly so simple.

A kill scene such as this is a sure indication of recent wolf presence.

Most people usually assume wolves control ungulate populations by how many they kill, yet the real controlling factor is usually the productivity of the land and climate fluctuations. A harsh winter might reduce moose or deer numbers, and then that in turn affects wolf numbers. So it is the deer that control the wolf numbers, usually, and it is usually weather that controls deer numbers.

Moreover, the notion of "balance" is misleading. In any particular predator-prey system at any given moment, it's not only possible but likely that the balance will not fit the theoretical ideal. That is, there will usually be too many predators or too many ungulates. The balance of predator and prey is best understood if one examines time in blocks of several decades, not several years.

THE HUNT

A wolf on the move is probably always hungry and probably always hunting. And wolves are on the move about eight hours of every day. Sometimes pack members lope along in single file, particularly when hunting in snow. At other times, packs fan out to cover more ground and improve the odds of flushing a victim.

Sooner or later, a pack member will see or smell an animal that might be prey. The pack then becomes excited,

Writer Barry Lopez suggests that a prey animal gives wolves permission to take its life.

although each wolf exercises restraint, moving forward with silent caution. Experience teaches wolves that they must be close to their prey before they can launch a successful attack. Wolves instinctively know better than to howl when stalking prey.

The most dramatic moment in the hunt occurs when prey and predator make eye contact. Wolves learn much by studying the response of their intended meal. Healthy, self-confident prey animals either flee or take a stand. Weak prey animals give signals that betray their vulnerability. Somehow, wolves can discriminate between the old bull moose that stands its ground because it can't run and the young bull that stands because it doesn't need to run.

Author Barry Lopez has written somewhat romantically about the moment when predator and prey study each other. Lopez calls this the "conversation of death." In effect, the wolf asks its prey, "Are you ready to die today?" The reply of a vigorous animal is "Hell, no!" But some animals cannot manage such a firm denial. Their body language reflects confusion, fear, weakness. Then the wolf presses the issue. Lopez even suggests that the prey animal gives permission for the wolves to take its life.

Biologists are more comfortable speaking of this encounter as a "testing" process. Testing often involves harassing prey animals to make them run. Injured, weak, or panicky animals betray their vulnerability. Wolves have an uncanny ability to detect the one caribou in a stampeding ocean that isn't running as fluidly as the others.

Lopez's "conversation of death" helps make sense of some cases of livestock depredation. Wolves sometimes run amok among livestock, slaughtering more animals than they could possibly eat. Centuries of domestication have turned livestock animals—which were once wild species—into dependent creatures with few natural instincts. When wolves challenge them, sheep and cattle panic, displaying exactly those signals given by wild animals that are distressed and unfit.

Biologists now talk about wolves "acquiring the prey image" for certain species. By that they mean wolves don't automatically recognize animals, even vulnerable animals, as prey. That explains the wolves that walk past sheep and cattle to hunt deer; they recognize deer as prey but might not recognize domestic animals the same way. But once a member or two of a pack has successfully killed an animal, the basic image of that animal is in effect held on file by the pack, and if they see that sort of animal again they go for it. As of the writing of this book, Yellowstone's wolves have not made a sustained, serious effort to kill the bison so abundant all around them, although they might soon.

Wolves almost always chase animals that run. Running implies weakness, and exposes the animal's vulnerable rump. An animal that holds its ground and maintains eye contact can stop a wolf pack in its tracks, although a small ungulate like a deer cannot stare down a wolf pack indefinitely.

During the initial rush, both the wolf and the prey reach for all the speed they can command. Most prey animals are quick enough to escape. Wolves make remarkably quick decisions about how likely their attack is to pay off. Their energy budget cannot afford many long, fruitless chases. They persist in long chases only when they have detected some hint of weakness.

Some hunts take a different course due to special circumstances. Moose, bison, musk oxen, and elk mothers vigorously defend their young. A wolf pack hunting a calf concentrates on separating the calf from its defender. Animals chased by wolves often run into water, where they make a stand or swim away to safety. If they can, wolves race around the shoreline to meet the swimmer when it tries to leave the water. Many winter kills take place on the ice, where wolves clearly have an advantage because they can maneuver better than their prey.

Moose are probably the most dangerous common prey of wolves. While most prey species depend on escaping, a healthy moose can usually fight off a wolf pack. Sometimes a bold wolf will grab the moose's sensitive nose. A wolf with a good nose grip can often control a moose, allowing the rest of the pack to swarm at its belly and hindquarters.

Contrary to common belief, wolves rarely hamstring their prey. Because the hooves are the ungulates' most dangerous weapons, wolves would routinely get their heads kicked if they tried to dive around the hooves to sever tendons. Wolves often attack high on an animal's rump—a big target and a safe place to bite. If a wolf can sink its long canines into that meaty rump, it can open a wound and perhaps knock the animal off its feet.

Nor is it common for wolves to use elaborate hunting strategies. Most chases involve a straightforward pursuit, with no decoys or ambushes. The issue is usually settled by speed and by how close the wolves are able to come before launching their attack. There is one possible exception. Observers have occasionally seen wolves working caribou herds with what appear to be more sophisticated tactics, such as driving caribou toward a wolf pre-positioned for ambush.

Researchers John and Mary Theberge have confirmed that the wolves of Algonquin Park occasionally fan out to hunt a broad series of ridges. The deer they jump will often run to icy lakes, where the wolf pack reforms to finish off the animal. This simple tactic improves the success of the pack.

Biologists get jeered by their peers when they anthropomorphize, but I'm just a writer so I'll say what they know but dare not say: Wolves love to hunt. Of course, a hungry wolf knows it must hunt in order to eat. But the emotional rush of finding, pursuing, and killing prey is enormously thrilling in its own right. Imagine being a wolf on the hunt, trotting mile after mile through a moonlit forest until you hit that ribbon of scent from an upwind deer. Imagine the stalk, the tension, the mad dash toward the bounding animal. Imagine the flying snow, the dangerous leap with snapping teeth, the hot blood steaming in the snow.

The joy of the hunt must be all the more satisfying because it's done in partnership with the rest of the pack. And after making a successful kill, it's easy to understand why a wolf would want to sit down, throw back its head, and . . . howl!

CHAPTER 7

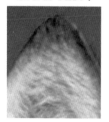

The Enigmatic Red Wolf

In 1624, eight years after his life was spared by Pocahontas, Captain John Smith published *A General History of Virginia*. In it, he said, "The wolves are not much bigger than our English fox." Smith was the first European to describe the red wolf (*Canis rufus*), the enigmatic wild canid of the American Southeast. He didn't seem to doubt that it was a wolf.

People have often doubted the designation since that time. Nothing about the red wolf has caused so much scientific confusion as its identity. Is it a wolf? If so, how does it differ from the gray wolf? Is the red wolf the sole survivor of a primitive race of wolves, or is it just a wolf-coyote hybrid?

These are not esoteric questions.

If you are a biologist dedicated to saving the last red wolves on earth, you worry about what a red wolf is because you need to decide which of the animals in your pens are wolves and which are wolf-coyote hybrids.

If you are a lawyer for the American sheep industry, you argue in court that the U.S. Fish & Wildlife Service (FWS) should not treat the red wolf as an endangered species because it isn't a species.

If you are an FWS manager, the issue is nettlesome because your agency isn't supposed to promote the spread of hybrids.

Putting aside that issue, the red wolf is fascinating because it was the first animal to make the transition from zoo animal to free-ranging predator, and the first carnivore ever to be reestablished in a range where it had become extinct. Efforts to save the red wolf led managers to pioneer a set of techniques later used to restore wolves to the Rockies and the Southwest.

The red wolf looks like a delicate version of the gray wolf. It also looks like a wolf/coyote hybrid. Adult coyotes weigh 20 to 50 pounds, adult gray wolves 70 to 110 pounds. At 50 to 80 pounds, the red wolf neatly splits the difference. The red wolf has a short

Scientists have debated: Is the red wolf a wolf, or is it in fact a wolf-coyote hybrid?

Pocosin Lakes
N.W.R.

Alligator River
N.W.R.

Great Smoky Mountains
N.P.
Cade's Cove Area

Estimated limit of the original red wolf range.

Area where last free-ranging red wolves lived before their removal.

Current (reintroduced) range of the red wolf.

coat, noticeably large ears, very long legs, a delicate frame, and a narrow muzzle. Many red wolves have a lovely copper coat flecked with dark guard hairs.

Debate about the identity and genetic history of the red wolf shows no sign of abating. Taxonomist Ron Nowak has argued the red wolf is not only a species but the original North American wolf. A recent study produced the stunning finding that the red wolf may be essentially the same animal as the wolf of Ontario's Algonquin Park; the two wolves certainly look alike, and now comparisons of their genes show great similarities. The Algonquin Park wolf, technically the eastern timber wolf, has always been considered a

The range of the red wolf has changed dramatically.

variant of the gray wolf. Now it might be lumped with the red wolf, so both would be *Canis rufus* or possibly both might be *Canis lycaon*.

Part of the problem is that there is no single accepted definition of what constitutes a "species." Nowhere is the matter of species differentiation as murky as in the world of canids, where wolves and coyotes and dogs can mate and produce fertile offspring.

But if taxonomists disagree about the red wolf's place in the world of canids, wolf biologists agree the red wolf is an important animal that absolutely deserves to be protected and restored to the wild wherever it is appropriate. Wolf biologists at a 1992 symposium decided to maintain the red wolf's status as a distinct species. A strong argument for that position comes from paleontological studies indicating that red wolves hunted the North American continent at least three-quarters of a million years ago. According to Gary Henry, coordinator of the FWS red wolf program, "If it is a hybrid, the red wolf is a 750,000-year-old hybrid."

In the words of Curtis Carley, a founder of the recovery program, "Whatever the red wolf is, the wolves we have . . . seem to breed true and

represent the southeastern canine that has been recorded as part of our past." Any animal that has been part of an ecosystem for 750,000 years has a strong presumptive case for belonging in that ecosystem.

THE RED WOLF

The red wolf once ranged over much of the southeastern quarter of the U.S. It lived as far west as central Texas and as far north as southern Illinois (or even southern Ontario, if Algonquin wolves are red wolves). In effect, the red wolf was the top canine predator of the southeastern forests, occupying the niche filled by coyotes in the desert West and gray wolves in the North.

Little is known about the habits of red wolves in the wild before restoration. By the time scientists took an interest in the 1960s, it was too late to begin field studies of the red wolf. The few remaining wolves were struggling to survive in wretched, atypical habitat, their social structures warped by the twin stresses of persecution and severely depressed population levels. Much of what biologists now know about the species comes from studies done on the first generations of red wolves reintroduced into the wild.

Because the first studies of red wolves were done of animals in marginal habitat, biologists thought red wolves preferred to prey on medium-sized mammals such as birds, nutria, and raccoons. When the first wolves released into the wild began hunting their own food, raccoons were a dietary mainstay. Since then, red wolves have become adept at preying on Virginia white-tailed deer, and Algonquin wolves occasionally take down a moose.

Studies on the first red wolves released in the wild have yielded other information. Researchers were surprised to discover that red wolves are quite social. Most had expected them to hunt individually or in pairs. But two-year-old and yearling red wolves frequently behave like young gray wolves, remaining with their parents to hunt, defend territory, and help rear the new pups. Pack bonding is especially strong at breeding time. The first red wolves to be reintroduced are defending territories of 20 to over 100 square miles. Red wolves are often described as more furtive and nocturnal than gray wolves.

THE DRIFT
TOWARD EXTINCTION

These shy little wolves suffered the fate of wolves everywhere when European settlers arrived and began remaking the face of the land. Settlers razed forest habitat and put the land to other uses. When unregulated hunting virtually eliminated white-tailed deer, wolves began preying on sheep and cattle. People retaliated. Wolves were shot, trapped, and poisoned until, in 1980, the species was declared extinct in the wild.

In the late 1960s, the red wolf made its last stand in 1,700 square miles of sodden marshlands in the shadow of giant petrochemical facilities along coastal Texas and Louisiana. This was vile wolf habitat. Wolves died from mange, hookworm, and heartworm. Mosquito populations were so high that calves in the area sometimes smothered from all the insects packed in their nostrils.

Things already seemed hopeless for the species when Texas biology professor Howard McCarley began calling attention to another threat: the last red wolves on earth were hybridizing with coyotes. As wolves were eliminated from the western portion of their historic range, coyotes expanded their range eastward.

Red wolf populations ultimately dropped so low that wolves began mating with coyotes, leading to what biologists call "hybrid swarm," the loss of species integrity through hybridization. The world's population of red wolves at this point was estimated at 100 beleaguered animals.

Even before there was a federal program to restore endangered species, biologists had begun listing the mammals they considered most at risk of extinction. The red wolf first appeared on that list in 1965. In spite of the listing, a federal predator control program continued to eradicate red wolves for another year.

When Congress passed the Endangered Species Act (ESA) of 1973, the red wolf was one of the first species listed. The FWS had already established a red wolf recovery program. It aimed to save red wolves in the wild by isolating the remaining wolves from coyotes. Trappers tried to maintain a coyote-free "buffer zone" around the last bit of wolf habitat.

The plan flopped. Federal trappers kept catching animals that they could not positively identify as true wolves or coyote-wolf hybrids. Because hybrids were such a threat to the remaining wolves, animals suspected of having coyote blood were

By the time scientists became interested in the red wolf, it was too late to begin field studies.

destroyed. It was a gut-wrenching task, because managers were killing animals that looked very much like red wolves at a time when the red wolf was the most endangered wolf in the world.

Ultimately, managers decided to remove red wolves from the wild in a last-ditch effort to save the species as zoo animals. That seemed to defy the ESA, which specifically charged the FWS with saving this endangered species in the wild. Even the managers who counseled this course wondered if they were making a terrible mistake. Said one: "We weren't sure we wouldn't be blamed for the extermination of the red wolf." Placing the world's last red wolves in cages to preserve them seemed to duplicate the notorious statement from the Vietnam War: "We had to destroy the village in order to save it."

Federal trappers collected over 400 wild canids, examined them, and sent those that looked like wolves—just 43—to a new captive breeding program run by the Point Defiance Zoo in Tacoma, Washington. Point Defiance was a progressive zoo with a strong interest in preserving endangered animals. That was a blessing, as no other zoo wanted these wolves.

Things went badly at first. Some wolves succumbed to diseases. Several were destroyed because researchers suspected they carried coyote blood. The number of healthy, genetically true red wolves slumped to a frighteningly low cohort of 14 wolves, and they weren't able to breed at first.

Just in time, the captive wolves began breeding. By 1992, the offspring of those 14 original animals numbered over 200 red wolves.

RESTORATION

When it became clear that the captive breeding program had saved the red wolf from genetic extinction, managers turned their attention to the next challenge. It was time to consider how and where a few wolves could be reintroduced to the wild. Managers faced two very different problems—one political and one biological. They weren't sure what set of techniques—which technologies— would allow zoo-reared animals to adjust to life in the wild. And they knew the whole program was likely to encounter political resistance.

Once again, early efforts were discouraging. A release planned for the Land Between the Lakes region of west Kentucky and Tennessee was dropped. The plan was firmly opposed

Managers placed red wolves in cages in order to save the animal from extinction.

by livestock and hunting groups, and it even drew criticism from environmental groups. Managers later concluded that bungled public relations had doomed the program. While disappointed, managers drew valuable lessons from the experience. Wolf restoration begins with education and good public relations.

To reduce public opposition, managers decided to take advantage of a 1982 amendment to the ESA. It created an option called the "experimental and nonessential" designation. This special designation allowed managers to conduct a species reintroduction without adhering to all the requirements of the original ESA.

For example, experimental and nonessential animals could be removed from the wild if they proved to be troublesome, an action not allowed under the original ESA. The designation also allowed managers to permit sport hunting in the release area, even if it might occasionally result in the death of a wolf.

The experimental and nonessential loophole was something of a two-edged sword, offering advantages but carrying risks. The wolves, which were undeniably highly endangered, would be turned out into the world with less legal protection than they would have had under the original provisions of the ESA. Under the

original ESA, even an animal that attacked livestock could not be killed.

The main advantage was that managers could deal with local citizens, including wolf opponents, in an atmosphere of more respect and cooperation. Opponents of an early attempt to reintroduce red wolves had argued, "We aren't against the red wolf, but we don't want all these stiff land-use restrictions of the ESA. And we don't want our cattle attacked by an animal we cannot touch because it is an endangered species."

Switching to the experimental and nonessential provision allowed wolf managers to reply, "Okay, we're reasonable people. If you leave our wolves alone, we'll not bring in all the restrictions usually involved with the ESA. And we will deal with wolves that cause trouble."

In a sense, this decision might be the most important legacy of the red wolf program because it directed wolf restoration away from the absolutistic and legalistic processes earlier used in ESA programs and moved it a long way toward pragmatism and cooperation. The decision created a sharp split in wolf fans between purists and pragmatists that continues to this day.

Where could the wolves be released? In 1984, an insurance company donated 118,000 acres of

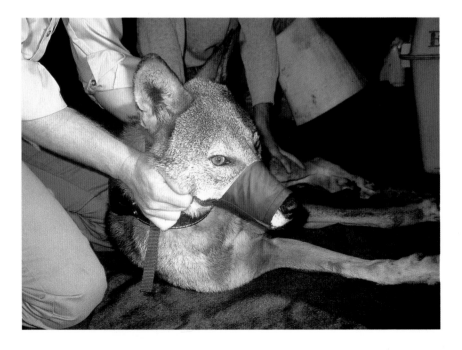

swampy land on the coast of North Carolina to the FWS. By happy coincidence, the new Alligator River National Wildlife Refuge (ARNWR) seemed ideal for red wolf reintroduction. The area was large enough, and it contained enough small mammals to support several wolf families. It was sparsely populated by humans. Best of all, the land had no livestock and no coyotes. Because the new refuge was a thumb of land surrounded by water on three sides, managers could prevent wolves from wandering into areas where they would conflict with humans.

The potential area for wolf releases was increased when a parcel of land known as the Pocosin Lakes region was acquired by FWS. Adjacent to the ARNWR, it offered 110,000 additional acres of wolf habitat.

Four pairs of red wolves were released into the ARNWR in 1987. It was the first reintroduction of an extirpated predator in the United States, and possibly the first in the world.

Because managers rightfully worried how a zoo-born predator would adjust to life in the wild, they developed a technique they called the "soft release." Soft release is a commonsensical protocol developed to ease the shocks of the transition of wolves to their new lives. The soft release allows the liberated wolves to gradually respond to the risks and joys of freedom.

Wolf families were confined in acclimation pens, where they could live in safety long enough to identify the local area as their home. Managers minimized contact with humans and even treated the wolves brusquely to discourage them from developing doglike bonds with humans. The wolves were gradually weaned from artificial food. The penned wolves were fed a diet of fresh carrion, primarily road-killed animals. Wolves were even given live prey, so they could practice killing their own food. Finally, the doors to the acclimation pens were opened, and red wolves were once again free to roam within at least a limited part of the Southeast.

LEARNING TO BE WOLVES

The red wolf reintroduction program was founded on a rather optimistic supposition: That a wolf reared in a zoo could learn to become a predator capable of killing its own food and withstanding all the threats of life in the wild. The first wolves to be released would be much like a family

Fish and Wildlife Service managers process a red wolf.

of humans crawling out of a bomb shelter after a nuclear holocaust. They would have no social support. They would know nothing about the world around them. They would have no skills for finding and killing food.

Managers were equally concerned about how well humans would tolerate the presence of wolves. It simply would not be possible for managers to protect the wolves from a hostile citizenry. There were too many people walking around with guns during hunting season and too many old logging roads on the refuge for managers

A moment of hope: Red wolves are released into the wild.

to patrol them all. If enough local people decided that red wolves were a threat, the wolves were doomed.

Between 1987 and 1997, 71 captive-born red wolves were released in the ARNWR. About 70 percent did not last long. They were hit by cars, killed by other wolves, drowned, or recaptured because they were too tame around humans. Wolves inclined to hang around people or their dwellings were removed before they could create problems. Some wolves just disappeared.

Those figures will sound discouraging, but only to people who aren't aware of the monumental challenges facing these zoo-bred wolves. It is hard enough to live as a wolf; to live as a wolf while you are trying to learn the trade of being a wolf is incredibly difficult. The more significant number is that in late 1998, 80 red wolves lived in the wild. Almost all of these free-living wolves are wild-born, and the wild-born wolves have predictably proven far more successful at living as a wild wolf.

Speaking off the record, one manager explained the program's success. "When you put zoo-bred animals in the wild, you know many of them are going to die. So you dump more wolves out there, and most of them die. And you dump more. Finally a few beat the odds and survive. They give birth to some pups. And when those wild-born wolves have pups, the pups are real wolves!"

Red wolf restoration managers rightfully consider their program a major success. Few wolves have been killed by people. Regional public opinion strongly favors the wolves, although the red wolf program continues to struggle with anonymity. Most of the red wolves now living in the refuge have never known life in a cage. Adult wolves are teaching youngsters how to live as a wolf, just as wolves have done for eons. A significant population of wild red wolves is living successfully in the Southeast again, and that is a minor miracle.

SMOKY MOUNTAINS NATIONAL PARK

A second reintroduction took place in 1991 in the southern Appalachians. Over several years, 39 wolves were released in the Smoky Mountains National Park.

This time, the reintroduction ran into trouble. Many wolves had to be recaptured after a short taste of freedom when they misbehaved, principally by straying onto nearby private land. Some wolves took up panhandling food in campground picnic areas. Several were shot, hit by cars, or poisoned (intentionally or unintentionally) with automobile antifreeze. No pups survived from the matings that were successful. Some pups died of canine parvovirus; others just died. Late in 1998, FWS reluctantly reeled in the remaining four wild wolves and declared an end to the program.

WHAT WENT WRONG?

First, the FWS always knew the Smokies would be a difficult test of the ability of their wolves to adapt. The reintroduction site was right near a large cattle operation, so this was considered a "worst case scenario" test from the start. For months, the wolves were amazingly well behaved, ignoring cattle and hunting wild prey. But when bad weather caused dead and dying calves to be dropped near them, the wolves discovered beef.

In effect, the land where the wolves were released failed to give them a fair chance at success in the wild. The land in the park has few recently logged-off areas, so many trees are old and large, which doesn't favor wolves or their prey. The Smokies, an ancient mountain range, features a lot of steep and eroded areas. Though the land makes a beautiful park, it could

not produce enough prey animals to allow wolves born in cages to succeed. When the wolves got hungry, they took off looking for more productive land, and that kept putting them on private property.

While disappointing, this was a learning experience for the FWS. For once, wolf restoration failed even though human intolerance was not a problem. Managers monitored the wolves tightly and recaptured most of them before they could cause trouble on private land. But in the end, the park simply didn't have enough good wolf habitat where captive-born wolves could learn to hunt, breed, and raise their young pups. Perhaps wild-bred wolves could have made it there, but not wolves born in zoos.

FWS managers have learned as much as possible from the experience. They are currently evaluating at least 26 new areas where wolves might be released more successfully.

THE FUTURE

Public antagonism could still cause problems for red wolves.

While the program has the support of as much as 80 percent of the public, it has acquired a few enemies, some of them politically well connected. Managers are encouraged by the recent creation of a private group, the

Red Wolf Coalition. They hope the Coalition can take the lead in winning public support for the program, leaving managers free to concentrate on working with the wolves.

Depredation problems have been minimal. The ARNWR wolves, especially the wild-born ones, have shown remarkably little tendency to assault livestock or pets. Even the wolves translocated to the Smokies behaved well until quirky weather taught them the joys of beef.

If the wolf of Algonquin Park does, in fact, prove to be the same animal as the red wolf, the red wolf restoration plan will experience some shocks. For one, the map of the red wolf's original range will have to be redrawn. The official goals of the recovery plan will need to be revised to take account of all those Canadian wolves. Perhaps the red wolf isn't really endangered, if it has a large pool of animals living in Canada. Currently, the whole program rests on the narrow genetic base of the 14 original red wolves trapped in the 1960s. For that reason alone, it would be wonderful if all the approximately 1,500 to 1,800 wild "red wolf type" Ontario wolves could become contributors to the red wolf program, either through breeding or by live-trapping and translocating them.

The researchers and managers who have guided the Red Wolf Program have come a long way, traveling mostly without a map. More challenges must be met before the program meets its ultimate goal of 330 wolves in captivity and 220 in the wild. The disappointment over the Smoky Mountains reintroduction effort should not obscure the towering fact that this pioneering effort in wolf restoration was extremely successful in spite of awesome threats.

The red wolf program tested two great questions whose answers were very much in doubt. The first was whether zoo-reared wolves would be too compromised by their artificial background to succeed in the wild. The second was whether humans could tolerate the close presence of red wolves. It would be impossible to say which challenge was greater: the radical attitudinal change being asked of people or the shock of liberation being experienced by the wolves.

So far, both people and wolves have performed better than just about anybody could have predicted two decades ago. The dramatic comeback of the red wolf, which transformed the species from a few extremely endangered animals in cages to successful, free-roaming predators, is a major triumph of wildlife management.

CHAPTER 8

The Gray Wolf of the Western Great Lakes

It turns out the math was simpler than we thought. We thought it was *tolerance + deer + wilderness = wolves*. But no, it turns out that *tolerance + deer = wolves*. If you've got enough deer and tolerance, the wilderness part isn't so critical.

Taxonomists thought the original wolf of this region was the eastern timber wolf, *Canis lupus lycaon*. They now believe it has always been *Canis lupus nubilis*, the Great Plains wolf. For reasons biological and political, scientists now downplay subspecies differentiations and talk instead about the "gray wolf," although residents still call their wolves "timber wolves."

The wolves of the western Great Lakes states range in size from 50 to 100 pounds, averaging about 70 pounds. Most are generally gray, although some have cream or black pelage. Since these wolves prey mainly on deer, packs typically include four to six wolves. Larger packs prevail in places where moose are the main food item.

Before these states were settled, wolf numbers were highest on the prairies, where stunning herds of bison, elk, and deer grazed. Since prairie wildlife was exposed and vulnerable to unregulated hunting, wolves and their prey were extirpated from the prairies in the nineteenth century.

But wolves hung on in the northern forests of Great Lakes states. After the great white pines were logged off, the second-growth forests that replaced them featured such brushy trees as aspen, maple, and birch. What had been moose and caribou habitat became superb white-tailed deer habitat. Wolves flourished in the new forests of the early twentieth century.

Wolf eradication was not quite the all-out war in the Great Lakes that it

The New World encountered by colonists was "the haunt of wolves and bears."

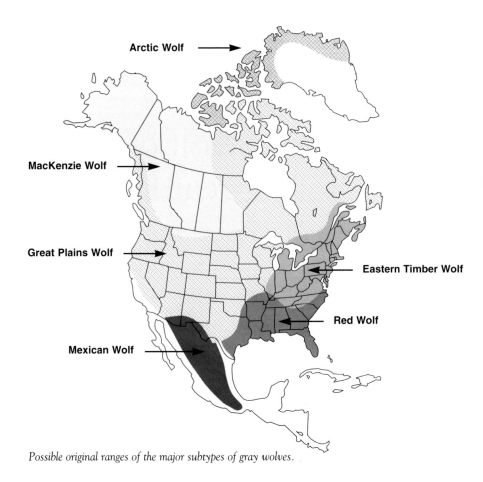

Possible original ranges of the major subtypes of gray wolves.

was elsewhere. In the West, the all-powerful livestock industry was dedicated to wolf eradication. By contrast, the northern regions of the Great Lakes states had mixed economies. The mining, tourism, and logging industries had no direct motive to per- secute wolves.

Even so, wolves were bountied and killed routinely. Wolves were killed for their luxurious pelts, but the main rationale for wolf eradication was the false hope it would lead to higher deer numbers. Deer were popular because

Wolf eradication never became an all-out war in the Great Lakes states.

they were a symbol of the north woods and the animal that made cash registers ring during hunting season. Unlike wolves, deer had obvious economic value.

When many Wisconsin deer began dying in the 1940s, biologist Bill Feeney organized a team of biologists to study the problem. Although Feeney knew Wisconsin's deer were starving because they had badly overbrowsed their range, he also knew the public blamed wolves. Feeney was so appalled at public hostility toward wolves that he kept his pioneering wolf study a secret and never let its

findings become known, even to other scientists.

By 1965, wolves had been extirpated from 97 percent of their original range in the lower 48 states. A remnant population estimated at 350 to 700 wolves lived in northeastern Minnesota, and a few lived on Isle Royale. Those few wolves were the pitiful vestige of a race of predators that once dominated the North American continent.

Then came the cataclysmic change. In 1974, the gray wolf received full Endangered Species Act (ESA) protection in the lower 48 states. The

Wolves have long been trapped for their hides, and destroyed as a means of managing moose and deer populations.

federal government, in the form of the U.S. Fish and Wildlife Service (FWS), assumed management control over gray wolves in all states except Alaska.

MINNESOTA

In the last year of Minnesota's bounty on wolves, anyone killing one was considered a local hero and rewarded with cash. Ten years later, anyone convicted of killing a wolf was a poacher who might receive a stiff fine. That abrupt change created a gap between federal law and local values, a gap felt with special resentment "up north" in wolf country where people prefer to run their lives with minimal governmental interference.

Wolf restoration requires an abundant supply of prey. Over-hunting and several successive harsh winters withered the Minnesota deer herd until it was in desperate shape in the late 1960s. In 1971, Minnesota's Department of Natural Resources (DNR) took the unthinkable step of canceling the deer season. The department then implemented a new and sophisticated deer program. When the timber industry invented a way to make money from aspen, formerly a "junk tree," logging increased dramatically. Forest management favored the cre-

ation of more young aspen stands, which produced a bounty of deer. By the early 1990s, Minnesota deer hunters were posting record deer harvests, year after year.

The dramatic resurgence of the deer herd helped wolves in two ways. All that venison generated legions of pups and dispersers. Just as important, anti-wolf spokesmen who had predicted wolves would "decimate" the deer herd lost credibility. Minnesota's record deer harvests came just when wolves were also reaching modern-time record levels. It was obviously possible to have excellent deer hunting and strong wolf populations at the same time.

Ultimately, the key to wolf restoration is wolf tolerance. Laws have little ability to protect a large predator like the wolf unless public opinion supports that animal. A symbolic turning point in wolf attitudes came in 1983, when the Science Museum of Minnesota mounted its exhibit "Of Wolves and Men." The show detailed the tragic history of wolf persecution and presented wolves in a more appealing light. Wolf hatred gave way to wolf acceptance . . . and even wolf adoration. Today the wolf is one of the most popular animals in Minnesota.

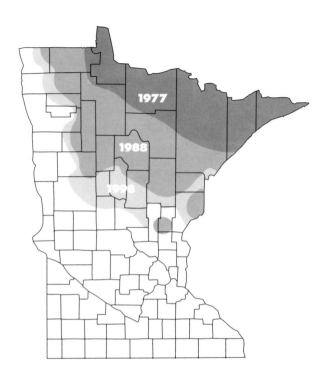

THE RECOVERY PLAN

Putting an animal on the endangered species list triggers a chain of events. One of the first steps is the FWS-supervised creation of a "recovery plan" for restoring that species to health. A special team, which included Dave Mech, created a wolf recovery plan in 1978. The plan was tweaked in 1992.

The team's first priority was to build the strength of wolf populations in Minnesota. Because a viable if small population existed, the team didn't need to arrange for expensive wolf transplants. The wolves would restore themselves if people would just quit killing them at such high rates.

The revised recovery plan established four management zones. Zones 1 through 3 had the most prey animals and acres of wild lands. Zone 4, considered marginal wolf habitat, includes many farms situated in

Wolves have steadily expanded their range in Minnesota since receiving federal protection. Wolf range is now approximately 40 percent of the state.

brushy land. Zone 4 is comprised of the kind of place where some livestock depredation is almost inevitable. Two-thirds of the state, Zone 5, is so highly developed that managers figured wolves wouldn't go there and wouldn't live long if they did. Altogether, the team felt that slightly over a third of the state (roughly the northeastern third) qualified as appropriate wolf habitat.

Three criteria were defined for delisting wolves and returning them to state control. First, the Minnesota population goal would be between 1,251 and 1,400 animals. Second, a viable population of at least 100 wolves must be created outside Minnesota but nearby. That population was expected to consist of the combined populations of Wisconsin and Michigan. And finally, all those counts must meet or exceed target levels for five successive years.

Wolves initially enjoyed total protection, although some were poached anyway. In 1978, the U.S. Fish and Wildlife Service downgraded the wolf's status from endangered to "threatened" in Minnesota (but not in Wisconsin and Michigan). That allowed authorized agents to remove Minnesota wolves that were responsible for killing livestock or pets. A 1998 FWS directive called for a reconsideration of the status of Great Lakes wolves because all delisting goals have been met and exceeded.

By 1998 the Minnesota wolf count had risen to 2,445 animals. In other words, Minnesota had almost twice the number of wolves needed to meet the minimum delisting goal. Wolf range consists of 40 percent of the state, with the size of permanent wolf range continuing to increase. Dispersers are showing up in areas where wolves were wiped out in the 1800s.

If people tolerate wolves, wolves tolerate people. Researcher Sam Merrill was jolted to discover wolves living comfortably in the middle of a National Guard training area an hour north of the Twin Cities. Multi-ton Abrams tanks rumble within yards of unconcerned wolves. Wolves lounge at rendezvous sites while Howitzer shells scream just over their heads. The wolves were smart enough to discriminate between a faux war and violence aimed at *them.*

The great expansion of wolf range is happy news for fans of wolves . . . but not necessarily for farmers who raise livestock in Zones 4 and 5, where wolves are now being seen for the first time in a century.

THE DEPREDATION PROGRAM

When wolves injure humans economically, people demand relief. Without a depredation program, aggrieved citizens take matters into their own hands, and such vigilantism often results in excessive wolf deaths.

It makes more sense and helps wolves more to create a program to minimize the economic losses caused by wolf restoration.

Minnesota's Wildlife Services (formerly known as Animal Damage Control) program is managed by the U.S. Department of Agriculture,

Wolf restoration in the Great Lakes area was relatively easy. All that was needed was to convince people to quit killing wolves at the rates they had been.

although funds come from the state. Some wolf advocates resent the agents of the program—after all, they are wolf killers—but the agents admire wolves and see their work as a critical element of the whole restoration process. Funding has at times been a problem because urban politicians fail to understand the need for wolf control or depredation compensation.

When a landowner complains about wolf depredation, an agent seeks evidence that a wolf was responsible. If the agent confirms wolf involvement, the offending wolf is trapped, and the landowner receives

Minnesota's surging wolf population marks this as the state to watch to see how well people and wolves can live together.

compensation. Some farmers are quick to "cry wolf." Since they receive no compensation for losses to coyotes or storms, they blame wolves whenever a calf or lamb goes missing. At the same time, wolves often remove or destroy the evidence of their attacks, making confirmation impossible.

Program agents would rather prevent depredation than deal with its gory consequences, so part of their work is educational. Sloppy animal husbandry can encourage wolf problems. If a farmer fails to dispose of cattle carcasses properly, wolves may discover the carrion and begin hanging around cattle. Similarly, it is dangerous for farmers in wolf range to allow cattle to drop their calves in isolated, brushy pastures. But wolves are tenacious predators, and even ranches protected by electrified wires and expensive guard dogs can suffer losses. Wolf fans who insist farmers are to blame for depredations have not considered the situation with an open mind.

Livestock producers criticize the program on three counts. They're frustrated when they lose an animal that can't be confirmed as a wolf kill despite abundant circumstantial evidence. Compensation payments were long capped at $400 per animal, which was often well below market value, but have recently been bumped up. Above all, livestock producers would prefer to forestall depredation by shooting wolves they see skulking around livestock *before* the wolves attack, but cannot do so under current laws.

A friend once attended a public hearing on wolf depredation. A farmer whose land included a major wolf travelway had suffered heavy cattle losses. He was accused of lying by a suburban woman who hated trapping. Her interpretation of Mech's research convinced her that a wolf pack could not eat as much beef as the farmer claimed he lost. The farmer sputtered in rage. He had been burying cattle ripped open by wolves, so there was nothing theoretical about the problem to him. Misunderstandings like this fuel wolf hatred and motivate farmers to defend their property with the old process of "shoot, shovel, and shut up."

Despite its limitations, the program is generally popular with landowners. They appreciate official acknowledgment of their losses, and they prefer receiving some compensation than receiving none. Objective observers consider it an important program that works fairly well.

Program reports make it clear that wild prey is the wolf's preferred food. Of all farms in wolf range, only about 2 in 100 experience confirmed wolf depredation. Yet some farms suffer significant losses. People who live in cities can be airily dismissive of the economic pain felt by rural families who live with wolves as neighbors. That pain can be real for some families.

A sharp increase in attacks on cattle and pets in the late 1990s left managers puzzled and concerned. Whereas agents only had been trapping about 40 to 50 bad-acting wolves a year, complaints became so frequent they had to trap 227 wolves in 1997. That number fell back to 161 in 1998.

There are three explanations. First, the brutal 1995-96 winter killed a great many deer, leaving hungry wolves scrounging for alternate food in subsequent years. Second, having saturated their prime habitat, wolves are dispersing into zones 4 and 5—those heavily settled areas where

Failing to fund or create depredation programs may be "anti-wolf," because it drives landowners to initiate their own wolf control programs.

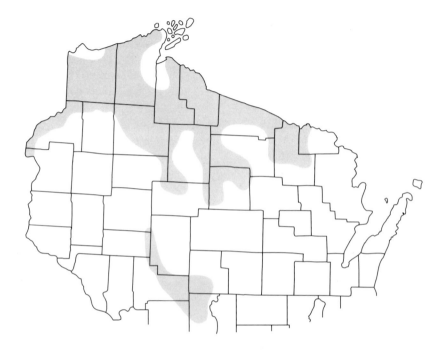

managers always knew wolves would get in trouble. Finally, decades of protection have taught wolves they have little to fear from humans. Wolves began showing up in small towns looking unconcerned, eating dog food from bowls left by houses and snatching suet balls left for birds.

Minnesotans might be dealing with a new animal, the *post-persecution wolf*. Researchers know a great deal about wolves that live in wild places and fear men. Less is known about this new bold wolf now showing up in small towns and little farm woodlots around the state.

WISCONSIN

Old Two Toes managed to survive in Bayfield County for several years in the 1950s, dodging bullets and eluding traps. Then during a snowstorm in

Wolf range in Wisconsin currently includes many areas of extreme northern Wisconsin, plus a separate population centered on the Black River State Forest.

1958, a car struck Wisconsin's last wolf on a road near Cornucopia, where my family has its cabin. He didn't die easily. The motorist twice battered Old Two Toes' skull with a tire iron and eventually slit his throat with a knife. The carcass was shipped off to Madison, where it is on display today. Old Two Toes was the last of Wisconsin's original wolves. The wolf was officially extinct in Wisconsin by 1960.

Wisconsin wolf managers knew the logical way to restore wolves was to let them disperse into the state from the expanding Minnesota population. Fortunately, there was a good path available to them in the lightly populated country south of Duluth and Superior. That's just where the "Stateline Flowage Pack" set up housekeeping. When dispersers from that pack trotted east into land rich with deer but free of wolves, they were the vanguard of Wisconsin wolf restoration and eventually Michigan's, too.

Population growth was slow but steady for years. Then came several agonizing years when almost no pups survived, apparently because of canine parvovirus. Wisconsin's wolves had to contend with distemper, Lyme disease, parvo, heartworm,

and mange—all potentially fatal afflictions that evolution hadn't prepared them to shake off. But the wolves apparently adjusted to parvo and pup survival improved.

The federal recovery plan set Wisconsin's population goal at 80 wolves. That goal was met several years ago. By 1998, the state's conservative count stood at 180 wolves in 47 different packs. Growth has been steady in recent years. Most wolves live in the top two tiers of northern counties, but they amazed observers by dispersing south to the Black River State Forest, where they appear to be doing well. Researchers calculate Wisconsin has enough wolf habitat to support about 800 wolves, if humans will tolerate that level.

People still shoot wolves illegally, but not as frequently as they did early in the program. A Wisconsin wolf now has a good chance of dying of natural causes. One radio-collared wolf lived to an estimated age of between 10 and 12 years. Very few wolves survive so long in the wild, where a wolf seven or eight years old is a senior citizen, often with gray hair to prove it.

An early issue with Wisconsin wolf restoration was highway development. Research showed that roads threaten wolves in two ways. Wolves like to travel roads and trails, which makes them vulnerable to being struck. Roads also open wolf territory to humans, increasing the risk of poaching.

Concern about roads diminished when further research showed that many wolves are casual about using and crossing highways. Roadless areas are still healthier for wolves, but some road-savvy wolves have discovered the smorgasbord of road-killed deer and raccoons found on highway shoulders.

The impact of wolves on the deer herd has always been controversial in Wisconsin. An adult timber wolf eats about 15 to 19 deer a year, some of them animals with injuries or weaknesses that doomed them to die whether a wolf came along or not. Wisconsin's 1998 wolf population might eat a little over 3,000 deer a year. Automobiles kill almost ten times that number. As long as the deer herd is managed sensibly, there will be more than enough deer for human hunters and wolves, with plenty left over for the cars as well.

Depredation complaints have been remarkably low, but are increasing as wolves disperse out of prime habitat into brushy cover near farms. A grow-ing problem has been attacks on dogs, especially bear hunting dogs, because they run around on their own, often far from their handlers.

Wisconsin's wolf program owes much of its success to outstanding public relations. Early planning emphasized public involvement. During three years of public hearings, managers practiced "conflict resolution" techniques. According to former wolf manager Dick Thiel, "It was hard to convince people that we were going to listen to them." People opposed to wolves kept assuming that managers "had a plan in their pocket," and were only going through the motions of seeking public input. Eventually, those participating in the debate realized that their involvement was meaningful.

Though Wisconsin's program is going exceptionally well, the long-range future of its wolves is not guaranteed. Much of the state's wolf habitat is fragmented. As people build more homes, cabins, and businesses in the northern counties, suitable wolf habitat will shrink. Another threat is the pressure to alter logging practices, which currently encourage young brushy timber. If more forests are managed as old-growth forests, Wisconsin's deer herd will shrink,

Managers have learned it is not necessary to have wilderness to have wolves. If people tolerate wolves and if the wolves can find food, they will live almost anywhere.

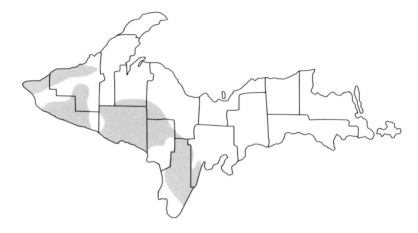

Michigan's wolf population has rapidly expanded throughout the Upper Peninsula and might even extend to the Lower Peninsula in the next decade.

dragging down wolf numbers. But as always, the biggest factor is human tolerance of wolves, and that is running high.

Wisconsin is creating a comprehensive state wolf management plan to replace the federal plan that is soon to be discontinued. Population goals for the state plan will be more conservative than the current federal goals. The state would be divided into three zones, with appropriate management measures tailored to the goals for each. When Wisconsin wolves are delisted by federal managers, they will be listed up by this progressive and protective state program until they satisfy its population goals and qualify for total delisting.

MICHIGAN

The last of Michigan's original wolves died in the early 1960s. Michigan's Upper Peninsula had a wealth of appropriate wolf habitat, but no wolves. An early experiment with the reintroduction of four Minnesota wolves ended quickly with four dead wolves. Ontario had wolves to spare, but there are no good travel corridors for Canadian wolves to reach the U.P. Michigan managers knew the best

Michigan and Wisconsin have strong and growing wolf populations. Of the two states, Michigan's U.P. is particularly blessed with good wolf habitat.

way to restore wolves to the U.P. would be to wait until enough dispersers made their way east from Minnesota or Wisconsin.

In the spring of 1991, Jim Hammill, Michigan's wolf biologist, confirmed the presence of a denning pack—the first wolves to den in Michigan in three decades. Numbers began to build. Remarkably enough, Michigan's wolves have increased at an average rate of 30 percent a year, which isn't very far below the maximum biological potential of wolves. That means that wolves are rearing full litters of disease-free pups, with very little additional mortality from humans. Perhaps dispersers from Wisconsin continue to add to the counts.

The count in the spring of 1998 stood at 140 adult wolves, with a strong cohort of pups coming along. That was a strong comeback after a 1997 count that was slightly below that of 1996, a response to problems in the deer herd after the severe winter of 1996-97.

Biologists estimate there is enough good wolf habitat in the U.P. to support 800 to 1,000 wolves. Much of the state's wolf habitat lies in large blocks that include extensive public lands, so Michigan's wolves might

have a better grip on the future than the wolves of Wisconsin. Additionally, wolves might soon find their way to the Lower Peninsula, where the howl of wolves has not been heard in a very long time.

With so much prime habitat to fill, wolves have not been forced to occupy marginal habitat where they are more likely to conflict with people. There were only four depredation claims in 1998, mostly on calves.

At this point, Michigan's wolf recovery program could hardly be going better. The population is strong and growing. Public acceptance seems good, although some deer hunters continue to grump that wolves are eating too many of "their" deer. The state has drafted a biologically sound management program that would maintain wolves on a state endangered list until the state's count holds at 200 wolves or more for five years.

ISLE ROYALE

Isle Royale is a beautiful, 45-mile-long island in Lake Superior that is

managed as a wilderness-style national park. The island lies just off the northeastern tip of Minnesota. Moose swam to the island in the late 1920s. With no predators to control their numbers, moose experienced an erratic boom-bust cycle for years. In the winter of 1949 an ice bridge connected the island to the mainland, allowing a wolf pack to migrate to the island and exploit its bounty of moose.

Researchers long ago recognized that Isle Royale could serve as a natural laboratory for studying predator-prey relationships. After four decades of continuous research, Isle Royale's wolf-moose system is the most thoroughly studied predator-prey relationship in the world.

Wolf and moose numbers have soared and dipped in complex patterns over the years. Moose populations have ranged from 500 to 2,500. Wolf numbers have been as low as a dozen and as high as 50. While humans often assume the predator—in this case, wolves—control how plentiful the prey will be, it is more accurate to say the number of vulnerable moose available at any moment controls how many wolves can survive. Ultimately, wolf and moose numbers are powerfully impacted by such factors as severe weather and the

condition of the browse on the island. A major lesson of all the research is that even a simple one-predator system is more complex than scientists expected.

The relative stability of this predator-prey system was shattered in the early 1980s when canine parvovirus hit wolves hard. Low wolf numbers caused moose numbers to multiply to levels never seen before, and the island's browse suffered long-term damage. Recently, though, wolves have rallied. From only 14 animals in the winter of 1997-98, wolves bounced back to 25 in the winter of 1998-99. Perhaps the system is moving toward stability again.

DELISTING

The recovery of gray wolves in the Great Lakes States is a triumph for the Endangered Species Act, for wolves, for managers, and above all for the good-hearted citizens of Minnesota, Wisconsin, and Michigan. Alas, the main beneficiary of the delisting process may be lawyers, as the decision to delist seems sure to be tangled up in the courts.

To sum up a complicated matter, several environmental and wolf advocacy groups are suspicious of the MN DNR and/or FWS. They announced

Despite an abundance of moose as prey, Isle Royale's famous wolf population is in serious trouble.

before the latest wolf survey was announced that they wouldn't believe its findings, choosing to believe there are fewer wolves and that those wolves are in more perilous condition than the DNR, federal managers, and neutral wolf biologists believe.

In addition to the wolf count, the second issue is the management plan the Minnesota DNR proposes to implement when it assumes wolf control. Delisting won't officially take place until federal authorities agree Minnesota has a plan that should keep wolves from falling onto the endangered species list again.

In an effort to thwart lawsuits, the DNR organized a panel of people interested in wolf management and asked them to propose a management protocol. The Minnesota Wolf Roundtable panel included wolf advocates, environmentalists, ranchers, hunters, managers, and outdoor writers. In addition to its own meetings, the Roundtable held a dozen public meetings around the state. What they encountered was a great deal of concern over wolf management, but little wolf hatred. Although a livestock group made inflated claims for wolf depredation, no group argued that wolves do not belong in Minnesota.

Even so, the group's discussions demonstrated a deep chasm in the

The wolf recovery team estimates that the eastern timber wolf will be delisted in 2005.

way wolves are viewed. For most participants, the wolf is a fascinating and highly valued member of the woodland ecosystem, but it is also an animal with a penchant for raising hell when it lives close to people. For wolf advocacy groups, the wolf is a symbolic animal, martyred through history, threatened by hatred now, and badly in need of their defense. Their emotional commitment to their position made political compromise almost impossible.

At a long and anguished final meeting, the panel members swallowed hard and endorsed a compromise management recommendation. It would allow wolves to spread throughout the state with no controls on numbers or where they would go. The compromise included a ban on hunting and trapping seasons for at least five years. Landowners would be able to shoot wolves caught in the act of attacking pets or livestock. The depredation program will be improved. Researchers will teach livestock producers how to minimize losses to wolves.

Most Roundtable participants believed a hunting season is needed, but they ultimately agreed it is too early to take that step. Both inside and outside Minnesota, there are many people who don't know how healthy the wolf population is. Many of them impugn the motives and professionalism of state and federal wolf managers. These people still regard the state's wolves as "endangered," and they can see no difference between old-fashioned wolf hatred and proposals for a hunting season. Some national wolf advocacy groups are so accustomed to fighting genuine wolf hatred that they fail to see the public in the Upper Midwest has accepted wolves to a remarkable degree. Meanwhile, wolves continue to suffer terrific persecution in the Southwest and parts of the northern Rockies. Although a strong biological case can be made for having a hunting and trapping season in Minnesota, Roundtable pragmatists realized that doing so would provoke a firestorm of criticism.

Why would the DNR want a hunting and trapping season? First, the department wants some device for limiting wolf numbers. The department is uncomfortable having no control at all over an animal that is increasing its population and expanding its range into settled areas. Second, the DNR and wolf biologists believe it is dangerous for wolves and for people when wolves lose their fear

of humans. When wolves fear people, people and wolves can coexist. When wolves grow bold, problems follow.

The DNR's model for what they would like is the state's black bear season. Bears, once shot on an unregu-lated basis as "varmints," have increased numbers since they began to be managed as a big game species with a limited seasonal take. But wolf fans cannot stand the thought of "going back to the bad old days of

Wolves have a secure place in the Great Lakes in the immediate future, although the long-term picture is less clear.

killing wolves." In the whole world of wildlife management, the two most inflammatory words are *killing wolves.*

If the Minnesota legislature accepts the Roundtable's proposed management program, resisting the temptation to fiddle, federal authorities will probably move to delist the gray wolf in the three western Great Lakes states and return management of wolves to the states. Wolves will no longer be on any list in Minnesota but would be protected by *state* "threatened species" listing in Wisconsin and Michigan. Given the health of wolf numbers, that would be entirely appropriate.

That should be a day for celebration, but wolf managers are already bracing themselves for the long, grueling court processes that seem sure to follow.

THE FUTURE

In spite of possible legal action, the success of wolf restoration in the Western Great Lakes states is a monumental accomplishment for all involved. With all trends looking so positive, it is hard to take a negative perspective on the future for wolves.

Yet the long-range prospects for wolves are not as happy as recent history might suggest. I personally anticipate that wolf numbers will build for a while, then reverse course and finally stabilize at a level close to or less than current levels. Why?

Wolves will flourish so long as they are given enough deer and human tolerance. The supply of both *could* go down in the future.

State DNR management policies favoring high deer populations are coming under heavy criticism. Environmental groups are raising lawsuits to force more management promoting old-growth forests. Old-growth forests produce few deer or other prey species, so wolf numbers might decline under new forest management protocols.

And as wolves occupy more and more highly settled areas, people who never thought about wolves are going to become highly concerned about them. The nature-loving people of northern counties in the three Great Lakes states have learned to put up with wolves. But when wolves show up in suburbs and small towns of corn country, the welcome mat might get yanked back. We have yet to see the limits of human tolerance of wolves seriously tested, and we surely will.

Still, the people of these Great Lakes states are never going to return to the old days of hating and routinely persecuting wolves. That is now unthinkable.

CHAPTER 9

Wolves in the Rockies

The original wolf of the northern Rockies might have been the *nubilis* wolf of the Great Plains, the larger *occidentalis* wolf of Canada, or possibly another subspecies now extinct. It doesn't matter. One researcher impishly named the wolf of this region *Canis lupus irregardless*, a Latinate way of saying, "a wolf is a wolf is a wolf."

What matters is that wolves have returned to the northern Rockies. Most spectacularly, wolves have returned to Yellowstone Park after an absence of about 60 years. The full story of how the wolf came back is harrowing and fascinating. It is a story with surprising villains and equally unlikely heroes.

THE GREAT CAMPAIGN

The effort to eliminate wolves in the West was often called a "campaign," and it was consciously likened to military combat. That campaign ultimately involved conventional, chemical, and biological warfare. In 1905, Montana cattlemen forced passage of a bill mandating veterinarians to infect wolves with mange and release them to infect others.

Much of the killing was done with strychnine. Millions of wolves and coyotes died, plus such unintended victims as badgers, foxes, and hawks. Cattlemen accidentally poisoned horses, cattle, dogs, and even a few of their own children.

Such an ugly campaign is easy to criticize today, but it arose from strange times. Market hunting had virtually extirpated wild ungulate populations by the turn of the nineteenth century. Wolves had no chance to make an honest living, so they turned to livestock. That made wolves the most hated enemy of the dominant industry in the West. The wolf was biting the rancher in his most sensitive spot: right on the wallet.

We'll never know how bad wolf depredation was because ranchers got in the habit of crying wolf whenever

The drive to eliminate wolves from the West was called a "campaign," and it was likened to military combat.

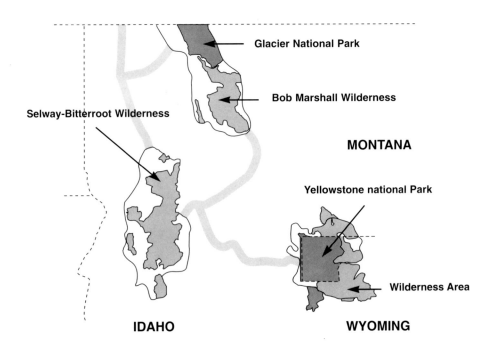

Glacier National Park

Bob Marshall Wilderness

Selway-Bitterroot Wilderness

MONTANA

Yellowstone national Park

Wilderness Area

IDAHO

WYOMING

they lost an animal to weather, disease, or accident. It sounded better to blame wolves than to admit to sloppy husbandry. But wolves were clearly a problem for ranchers in this era of ecosystem unbalance.

Viable wolf populations disappeared from most western states and their big parks in the 1920s. By the 1930s, the howl of the wolf was no longer heard in the West.

**THE WOLF
THAT KEEPS SHOWING UP**

Wolves remained absent from the Rockies for half a century. Now and then, somebody glimpsed a wraithlike shape that might have been a wolf. These shadowy reports increased in the 1970s, convincing biologists that dispersers from Canada were filtering into the empty habitat. But those lone wolves weren't meeting other

Rocky Mountain wolf recovery area and possible dispersement corridors.

wolves and forming packs. And in spite of being protected by the Endangered Species Act (ESA), they were not surviving long.

In the early 1980s, researchers confirmed the existence of a wolf pack in Glacier Park, the first U.S. pack to exist outside Minnesota and Isle Royale. Those first arrivals must have thought they had dispersed their way into wolf heaven. Glacier held bountiful herds of fat deer that were living a sort of Disney animal's life, blissfully unaware of the existence of wolves. Glacier's wolf population began increasing at a rate of 40 percent per year, which approaches the fastest expansion the wolf's biology permits.

The wolves of northwestern Montana did exceptionally well until the notorious winter of 1996-97 killed 70 percent of the area's white-tailed deer. Wolf numbers dropped in response to this sharp reduction in available food. Parvovirus might also have limited pack sizes. By 1999, there were about 88 wolves in five or six packs in northwestern Montana. Wolf numbers are expected to rise again when the deer numbers recover.

Once established in Glacier, wolves began traveling southward along the spine of the Rockies with increasing frequency. Today they're showing up in all sorts of places. A small pack has denned more or less continuously in Montana's Ninemile Valley since 1990. But wolves dispersing from Glacier tend to land in areas with many cattle and few wild ungulates, so they often get into trouble. Depredation control agents have removed several of the wolves that dispersed from northwestern Montana.

A separate but much smaller migration has occurred along the western slope of the Rockies. Wolves have trickled out of British Columbia into empty habitat in Washington. But these dispersers are not numerous enough and are not surviving long enough to meet and form packs.

There is organized interest in returning wolves to the Olympic Peninsula of Washington, but it won't happen soon. Public meetings have made it clear that wolves won't be welcomed until wolf advocates do more education and public relations work.

THE GREAT YELLOWSTONE DEBATE

The great public debate on wolf restoration in the West has centered on Yellowstone Park, the nation's oldest and most famous park. The

Yellowstone wolf controversy acquired the status of one of the most dramatic wildlife management disputes of our century.

This debate was actually two fights. First and most conspicuous was the fight between wolf advocates and wolf opponents, between those who believed Yellowstone without wolves was a tragically incomplete ecosystem and those who believed returning wolves to the West would be a tragic mistake. The second fight was between two feuding wolf advocacy groups, groups we can characterize as purists and pragmatists.

Perhaps the first voice asking for a return of wolves to Yellowstone was Aldo Leopold's. Arguing in 1944 against the ignorance of questioning the economic "worth" of individual species, Leopold explained that an

Wolves suddenly seem to be materializing throughout the Rockies.

ecological system is meant to function as a whole; thus each piece has its essential role to play and is inherently valuable. This concept would not catch on with progressive naturalists for another three decades, and it seems unlikely that the average American understands it yet.

When the Endangered Species Act was adopted, the U.S. Fish & Wildlife Service (FWS) became responsible for preparing plans to restore wolves in the Rockies. Early efforts were marked by bureaucratic timidity that, in retrospect, was politically realistic. The powerful livestock industry hated the wolf and the general public feared the wolf. As long as that was true, wolf restoration was going nowhere.

But the ESA is a strange and stubborn law. It put in motion some machinery that took on a life of its own. As word leaked out about early restoration plans, the great battle began to take form. Wolf opponents began to issue foolish statements. Wolf proponents began to make the case for the wolf. Each side goaded the other on.

Increasingly, the fight centered on returning wolves to Yellowstone. Typical of arguments for wolf restoration is the comment by John Varley,

chief of research at Yellowstone in the early 1980s. "If we restore wolves to Yellowstone, it will be the only place left in the 48 states that has all of the native animals and plants that were here when white men hit the shores of North America. Now there are none. Why can't we have just one place like that?"

Environmental groups made the Yellowstone wolf restoration a showcase issue because it was the most crucial test to date of the ESA. Wolves were once the keystone predator of Yellowstone. The park had functioned

As illustrated by this poster, anti-wolf sentiment remains strong in the West.

for years without significant predation on large ungulates, but now was badly out of balance as a result. If wolves could be barred from a place in which they so obviously belong, the ESA would be reduced to being a paper tiger. Conversely, if the nation's most controversial predator could be restored in such a prominent location, the ESA would emerge stronger than ever.

The fur really flew when the FWS finally issued a draft restoration plan that would restore wolves to the northern Rockies, including moving wolves to Yellowstone.

Several western congressmen distinguished themselves by spouting irresponsible and ignorant proclamations. A Montana senator predicted that, if wolves returned to the park, "There'll be a dead kid within a year." An Idaho senator informed schoolchildren that wolves "pose a real danger to humans." Western national politicians adopted the slogan of the arch-enemy of the wolf, the American Farm Bureau Federation, swearing there would be "no wolves, nowhere, no how!"

Wolf advocates retaliated with public education efforts, and they began to win important victories. In 1985, the Defenders of Wildlife brought the "Wolves and Humans" exhibit from St. Paul's Science Museum to Yellowstone Park. Thousands of visitors found its message compelling. In polls, Yellowstone visitors favored wolf restoration by a six-to-one ratio. Polls in Idaho, Montana, and Wyoming showed majority support for returning wolves to the park.

For wolf advocates, the great Yellowstone fight felt like rolling a boulder up the steep slope of a mountain. Each triumph over a major obstacle was rewarded with a new obstacle. Opponents called for hearings to prove that local people didn't want wolves. Most attendees at the

hearings supported wolf restoration. Unhappy with that result, opponents called for more meetings to be held in towns where wolf opposition would be sharper. Once again, most attendees supported wolves.

Politically appointed high-level FWS bureaucrats said wolf restoration would have to wait until studies could evaluate the potential impacts of wolves on Yellowstone and its environs. The studies kept finding that Yellowstone, with its dangerous overabundance of elk and bison, was a place begging for a predator like the wolf. "That's interesting," said the bureaucrats, "do another study!"

Strong leaders in the U.S. Park Service and FWS lost their jobs from time to time when their wolf advocacy offended politically powerful groups. They were replaced by people opposed to wolves or at least very skeptical about them. Oddly, some of them changed their minds as they worked with the issue. When it was clear they had lost the contest for the public's heart and mind, wolf opponents turned again and again to the courts to block wolf restoration.

Complicating the challenge for wolf advocates was the retreat of the Republican Party from environmental values. In the 1970s many promi-

After all the legal and political fighting, the actual process of restoration in the Rockies went amazingly well.

nent Republicans helped pass the ESA and other landmark environmental measures. By the 1980s, particularly in the West, Republican national politicians sided with extraction industries and the so-called "wise-use" lobbyists. The West had become a one-party region, and that party was increasingly hostile to environmental values, especially wolf restoration.

In the end, the unlikely decision of Idaho Republican Senator Jim McLure to sponsor wolf reintroduction legislation broke the deadlock. McLure might have felt livestock interests would be better protected by grudging cooperation than adamant opposition. He has never explained just what his motivation was.

DEFENDERS DEPREDATION FUND

Opposition to wolves in Yellowstone centered on the fears of ranchers that wolves would flee the park and begin attacking livestock all over the West. Wolf supporters admitted that some wolves—not many, but some—might disperse from the park, and some of them might attack cattle or sheep.

Wolves might have naturally recolonized Yellowstone National Park but the decision was made to import them.

Ranchers were irate because wolf fans, many of whom live in distant urban areas, were dictating wildlife policy in the West, but it would be Western ranchers who would lose income to wolf depredation. While wolf advocates believed depredation would be minimal, some were uncomfortable about the injustice of having ranchers bear the whole economic burden of wolf restoration.

The breakthrough came when William Mott, director of the National Park Service, suggested to Hank Fischer of Defenders of Wildlife that the single most important action conservation groups could take would be to develop a fund to compensate ranchers for any livestock losses caused by wolves.

By 1992, Defenders of Wildlife had created a $100,000 fund to pay for verified stock losses to wolves anywhere in the northern Rockies. The program has been expanded and improved in several ways since then. In a typical year, it now pays out about $30,000.

Ranchers have mixed feelings about compensation. Because of their independence and pride, they would much prefer to *prevent* depredation by eliminating wolves that seem to pose a threat to their operations. Yet they appreciate not being stuck paying the whole bill for other people's wildlife values. If nothing else, the depredation fund is a gesture of respect and concern, and it takes much of the economic sting out of wolf restoration.

Creation of this program did at least two things. It blunted the sharp edge of resistance to wolves among livestock producers, and it helped wolf advocates as they made the case for wolves in legal proceedings.

IMPORT OR WAIT?

Meanwhile, wolf advocates had a vigorous fight within their own ranks. As so many of these issues do, this one split along familiar lines. One side was pragmatic, accommodating, and more trusting of the general public. The other side was more legalistic, inflexible, and suspicious of all the people who hated wolves.

Through the long process of policy formation, FWS managers had identified three regions where wolves could be restored and expected to thrive with minimal conflict with humans. One was where wolves already existed, in northwestern Montana around Glacier Park and the Bob Marshall Wilderness Area. The second area was a large chunk of excellent habitat in central Idaho, land containing the

Selway-Bitterroot Wilderness area. Third, but symbolically most important, was the greater Yellowstone Park ecological area.

After wolves discovered the bounty of venison in the Glacier area, they began to sporadically show up in Idaho in the 1980s, and there were documented sightings of mated pairs. Wolves were possibly sighted in Yellowstone at the same time, although those sightings were controversial and fleeting.

Everyone agreed that wolves would discover the superb habitat managers wanted them to reoccupy. It was just a matter of time, but how much time? And what was the management protocol most likely to help them succeed?

Many environmental purists felt the best restoration plan was to exercise patience and let the wolves do the job on their own. That would avoid all the business of trapping wolves and decorating them with collars and ear tags. It would be natural. It would avoid the spectacle of the intrusive federal government forcing wolves on the West. Best of all, the wolves would come in as endangered species, with full ESA protection. Nobody could kill them.

Pragmatists argued the other side.

Researchers said it might take 40 years before Yellowstone could lure in enough wolves to let them form packs and begin procreating. Moreover, they said, the inflexible character of the ESA would poison the well of public opinion by making it impossible for managers to remove a wolf that was attacking livestock. By using the "experimental and nonessential" provision of the ESA, wolves could be brought to Yellowstone and Idaho *soon* and under more flexible management provisions that would give the FWS a chance to work cooperatively with ranchers.

Committed, intelligent people argued forcefully on both sides . . . and continue doing so to this day.

THE PLAN

After years of battles, meetings, and analyses, FWS adopted a restoration plan and ushered it through the various challenges and stages of approval. Briefly, it identified the three regions where wolves could be expected to thrive without conflicting with people. The goal is to have 10 breeding pairs in each of those areas for three successive years. At that point, which might come as soon as 2005, wolves would be delisted and turned over to state control.

The pragmatists won the day on management protocol. Canadian wolves would be translocated under the relaxed ESA standards. In effect, wolf advocates offered to strike a bargain with the livestock industry: Let us have wolves, and we'll give you protection against depredation. If some of our wolves misbehave, we'll move or destroy them.

Wolves that stay inside the three management zones are now fully protected. Wolves that disperse out of the protected zones, even those dispersing out of Glacier, are considered "experimental and nonessential" and thus vulnerable to control if they attack livestock.

HELICOPTERS AND KENNELS

In December 1994, Canadian trappers began collecting wolves from an area of Alberta not far from Jasper National Park. Weeks later, helicopters swooped low over brushy islands, flushing wolves into the open where the choppers, flying dangerously close to the ground, could give dartgun marksmen a clear shot.

Wolves translocated from Canada to Yellowstone would not be familiar with the park's unusual terrain.

Wolves were processed in a variety of ways, mostly for research. They were innoculated, weighed, tagged, analyzed for age and pack role, and fully documented.

On January 12, 1995, 8 wolves in aluminum kennels were brought into Yellowstone. After a last-ditch legal maneuver failed, they were released into acclimation pens in family groups. Days later, 4 wolves were hard-released into central Idaho. Soon afterward 11 more wolves were released on the Middle Fork of the Salmon River. Late in March, 14 wolves were released from their acclimation pens to go free in Yellowstone. Over two years, 33 Canadian wolves were released in Yellowstone.

THE SWEET SMELL OF SUCCESS

And they prospered.

Researchers have likened the fate of those wolves translocated to Yellowstone to "winning the wolf lottery," because the park was packed with ungulates, especially 30,000 to 40,000 predator-ignorant elk. The new wolves quickly began to whittle down the bloated elk herd, restoring balance to the park. By 1999, Yellowstone had about 115 adult wolves, with at least 10 pairs raising litters.

So far, elk constitute 90 percent of the wolves' diet. Managers hope wolves will learn to take on the park's overly abundant bison, but few wolves have challenged the powerful and cantankerous bison, probably because the equally abundant elk are less threatening to hunt.

Yellowstone's wolves are thriving. Wild wolves are usually lean, if not gaunt. The wolves of Yellowstone are butterballs, relatively speaking. Because food is so plentiful, packs defend territories a third as big as would be normal. Wolves have increased at rates rarely seen.

One happy surprise is that the wolves have been highly visible. At least 10,000 visitors each year are seeing wolves, leading to an entirely new brand of Yellowstone tourist. Families are coming great distances to enjoy "wolf vacations" as they squat behind spotting scopes and watch wild wolves living naturally in spectacular scenery.

Park wolves have strayed less than managers had predicted, probably because so much food is available in the park. Wolves have moved into the Jackson, Wyoming area. The famous Soda Butte pack found the nearby National Elk Refuge, giving even more tourists the chance to watch wolves hunt elk.

Although nearly all park wolf packs live near livestock, depredation has been less than expected. Each year, managers have had to deal with about four or five wolves that acquire the habit of attacking cattle.

The Idaho wolves are succeeding even better in terms of numbers. By 1999, Idaho had about 120 wolves including 10 to 13 breeding pairs. The Nez Perce tribe asked for and received permission to manage Idaho's wolves, and have done an outstanding job. The tribe has a strong cultural association with wolves. These wolves are not tangling with cattle and sheep, although some hunting outfitters are worried they will reduce elk numbers.

Wolf restoration in the Rockies took place just when the Internet had become popular, and now at least two superb web sites track the activities of these wolves with loving detail. Because of the intense interest in these wolves, fans can follow not only the fate of individual packs but each individual wolf. Strong interest in the wolves in Idaho resulted in schoolchildren naming Idaho's wolves.

STORM CLOUDS

Just as wolf fans were savoring their great success, a new threat came from an unanticipated quarter.

Two lawsuits opposing the wolf program went before Wyoming's Judge William Downes. One was brought by the American Farm Bureau, and it argued that the wolves should be removed because the "true" wolf of the Rockies, *Canis lupus irremotus*, still existed in the Park as a few isolated individuals that would be genetically swamped by Canadian wolves of the wrong subtype. A suit brought by several environmental groups who opposed the pragmatic, looser protection of the FWS plan argued that this lax level of protection was endangering wolves that had naturally migrated into the management zones.

To the astonishment of all observers, Downes joined the suits of the wolf-haters and wolf-advocates, then concluded the whole reintroduction program violated the ESA. Those Canadian wolves would have to go.

Go where? Canada won't take them back. No state can accept 200 to 300 wild wolves. FWS managers insisted their program had been biologically and legally sound, and vowed to defend it vigorously in court. If they lose, helicopter gunships would be sent out to destroy the wolves that so many people worked so hard to bring back. The decision is under appeal.

Wolf fans cling to the conviction that such an outcome is literally unthinkable in this age; that surely, one of the greatest victories of wildlife management cannot be turned into a tragedy this way.

CHAPTER 10

The Lobo

The first 11 wolves reintroduced to the Southwest in 1998 probably never had much of a chance. They had lived their whole lives in captivity. They didn't know how to identify, find, or kill their own food. Nor did they know anything about the world into which they were released—such as where water might be found, where deadly cougars lurk, or where roads enable humans to enter their world.

Worse, in spite of efforts to prepare them for this cataclysmic life change, these captive-raised wolves were clueless about how dangerous humans can be. Some wolves might have associated people with food instead of death. A biologist in the program ruefully called them "knucklehead wolves." Under the best of circumstances, many of them were likely to die.

They did not get the best circumstances.

The 11 Mexican wolves were not just released into the wild, they were inserted into the middle of a war between the Old West and the New West. The wolves landed on ground bitterly contested by ranchers and hunters on one side and environmentalists and recent migrants on the other. Recent federal decisions to restrict grazing rights and cut back on logging had, in the minds of many residents, threatened the economic stability of the region and cast all federal authorities in a bad light.

Moreover, these highly endangered wolves were released into a piece of land open to hunting. Unlike Yellowstone or Glacier, the Blue Range Primitive Area of eastern Arizona and western New Mexico is a free-fire zone for anyone who wants to shoot a coyote, and the ground is liberally cross-hatched with roads. Shooting coyotes is almost a reflexive response for many Southwesterners, and no supbspecies of gray wolf resembles the coyote so much as the Mexican wolf.

Less than a year after their release, none of the original 11 still lived in the wild. Necropsies on the bodies of

The lobo is the most endangered wolf in North America.

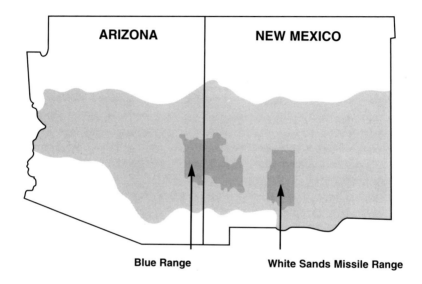

ARIZONA　　　　　NEW MEXICO

Blue Range　　　　　White Sands Missile Range

five wolves showed they died from shots from several different rifles. Another wolf was missing and presumed dead. The others were recaptured and returned to confinement, either because they had not worked out well in the wild or for their own protection.

For the people who had worked so hard to return the wolf to the Southwest, the failure of the first release was sickening but not entirely disheartening. Although nobody knew if the shootings were random events or the result of a conspiracy, FWS officials made it clear early on that they would continue releasing wolves until the program worked.

"This reintroduction is going forward," said Interior Secretary Bruce

The major area for Mexican wolf restoration is a section of land straddling the Arizona-New Mexico border called the Blue Range area, although the White Sands Missile Range is still being considered.

Babbitt, himself the son of a Southwest ranching family. "The wolf is back. It's here to stay."

THE UNIQUE LOBO

E. A. Goldman, wolfdom's consummate taxonomic splitter, believed there were once five races of wolves inhabiting the Southwest. That degree of complexity was almost surely too fussy, but it doesn't matter, since four of Goldman's five southwestern wolves are extinct. We are left with but a single southwestern race of gray wolf—*Canus lupus baileyi*, the Mexican wolf or lobo. Unfortunately, the precise history of the different wolf races is one of many issues that biologists can't properly research, because no objective studies were done before it became too late.

The Mexican wolf is the smallest gray wolf in America, weighing from 50 to 90 pounds. Mexican wolves differ from northern wolves by virtue of shorter coats and more pointed ears (two adapations for warm weather), and a tendency toward ruddy pelage color. The lobo looks more like a coyote than other gray wolves, both in size and general conformation.

A genetic analysis of Mexican wolves conducted in the early 1990s surprised researchers. Their DNA contains a unique pattern, which makes a strong case for considering the Mexican wolf a distinct subspecies of gray wolf. This finding led an international council of wolf scientists to call the Mexican wolf the "highest priority need for wolf conservation the world over."

HISTORICAL PERSPECTIVES

According to historical accounts, wolves were relatively scarce in the Southwest when European settlers arrived. That makes sense since much of the region consists of arid plains that could not support enough ungulates to feed many wolves. The lobo was primarily an animal of montane forests, those relatively moist and thickly forested watershed regions on the gentle slopes of mountain ranges.

Everything changed when European settlers arrived. They badly overhunted mule deer, elk, and the small Coues white-tailed deer. Many wild ungulates were shot by market hunters supplying meat to booming mine towns. Settlers then filled the plains with cattle and sheep. "By the late 1880s," writes historian David E. Brown, "the Southwest was one large livestock ranch." Deprived of natural food, wolves began exploiting all the bovine protein they found around them. Wolf numbers might have increased as wolves fed on the poorly guarded herds.

The period that followed was curious. Never, before or since, were so many predator exterminators employed to destroy so few animals in order to produce such dubious benefits. Federal "wolfers" in the Predatory Animal and Rodent Control (PARC) program routinely exaggerated the economic impacts of wolf depredation and even exaggerated the size of the animals they destroyed. National Park Service officials, eager to win support for the newly formed agency, joined in the great campaign to rid the Southwest of wolves, bears, and mountain lions.

As wolf populations fell, the last survivors became extremely wary. Several wolves gained notoriety, much like human outlaws on the "ten most-wanted list." They had been given names: Las Margaritas, Old One Toe, the Chiricahua Wolf. When one of these famous cattle-killers was destroyed, newspapers trumpeted the news all over the Southwest.

Above: A Mexican wolf strolls through simulated natural habitat.
Right: The Mexican wolf is the smallest American gray wolf, and it generally shares some features and coloration with coyotes.

Despite sensational tales about ghostly, uncatchable individuals, the wolf was not difficult to eradicate. In just 11 industrious years, PARC agents eliminated viable wolf populations throughout the Southwest. The program continued in a "mopping-up" mode for several more decades.

The last wolf killing in the American Southwest had the quality of a political assassination. In the mid-1970s, what came to be known as the "Aravaipa wolf" was sighted several times in mountains west of Sulphur Springs, Arizona. When the Mexican wolf was placed on the list of endangered species, ranchers feared that the Aravaipa wolf might become the founder of a resurgent wolf population. Arizona stockmen quietly put the word out that they would pay a bounty to anyone who took care of the problem. The Aravaipa wolf became the first wolf to die as a direct consequence of the Endangered Species Act (ESA).

DODGING THE BULLET OF EXTINCTION

The Fish and Wildlife Service (FWS) listed the Mexican wolf as an endangered species in 1976. Unlike the gray wolf, which in the 1970s was endangered in the United States but prolific in Canada, the Mexican wolf was highly endangered in the genetic sense. This subtype of gray wolf faced extinction because there was no known, viable wild population anywhere that could be tapped for a recovery program.

In 1977, the FWS hired Roy T. McBride, a famous wolf trapper, to live-trap as many wild lobos as possible. McBride eventually caught five wolves in the Durango region of Mexico. Only one was a pregnant female. Ultimately, four wild wolves became the seed stock for the captive breeding program.

Those lobo bloodlines were eventually enriched when genetic analyses showed that several wolves in zoos were Mexican wolves and could be added to the program. The "Aragón" and "Ghost Ranch" bloodlines added badly needed diversity to the program's foundation stock.

Although tantalizing rumors persist that wild lobos still live in remote areas of Mexico, many years have passed without confirming their presence. Researchers now doubt there are viable populations of Mexican wolves in the wild, although they continue to hope they are wrong.

For several years, the captive breeding program did little more than tread water, keeping the lobo alive genetically. The number of Mexican wolves in zoos remained low because there was no place to put more of them.

DELAY AND RECOVERY

In 1979, the FWS created a Mexican Wolf Recovery Team. The agency produced a recovery plan that was signed by U.S. and Mexican officials in 1982. The team did not have many management options. It could not hope that wolves would naturally recolonize old habitat. Wolves could be restored to the Southwest only if people put them there, using the relaxed regulations of the ESA's "experimental and nonessential" clause to minimize conflicts with livestock producers.

For several years the Mexican wolf recovery program lay dormant. The FWS could have prepared the groundwork for wolf recovery in the early 1980s by conducting public information and education projects. But the service did virtually nothing because it lacked funding and—according to some of its critics—because senior officials were reluctant to push an unpopular project.

Finally in 1986, local and national pro-wolf groups pressured FWS to fulfill its responsibilities under the ESA. The FWS asked the wildlife agencies of the three states to propose possible reintroduction sites. Texas stonewalled, claiming that there was no place in the entire state suitable for wolves. Arizona offered 15 sites. New Mexico offered one site, White

Sands, a 4,000-square-mile facility used by the U.S. Army as a bombing practice range.

Naming White Sands as a possible site galvanized opposition to the Mexican wolf program. Livestock owners and hunting groups organized to block wolf restoration. In 1987, in the midst of the debate, an Army commander flatly announced, "We do not want wolves on the White Sands Missile Range." The regional FWS director stunned pro-wolf groups by announcing, "The wolf reintroduction program, as of now, is terminated."

ADVOCACY GROUPS

Wolf advocacy groups rebounded. They formed the Mexican Wolf Coalition, which sued the departments of Interior and Defense for failing to implement the ESA. The logjam broke. The Army reversed its opposition to wolves on White Sands, although FWS later decided White Sands didn't hold enough food to support many wolves. Wolf educational materials developed by the FWS but never released were finally put into circulation. Congress appropriated a modest amount of money for Mexican wolf reintroduction.

None of the progress would have been possible without stout advocacy from both national and local wolf groups. Although distracted at first by the Yellowstone fight, the Defenders of Wildlife finally made the lobo's plight a priority. Strong local Mexican wolf committees—particularly P.A.W.S., an Arizona group headed vigorously by Bobbie Holoday—raised thousands of dollars and conducted public information projects. In effect, wolf advocacy groups stepped into a vacuum and built support for the wolf.

One event demonstrated what can happen when bitter partisans give dialogue a chance. In 1991, Defenders of Wildlife's Hank Fischer addressed a meeting of the Arizona Cattle Grower's Association. Rather than castigating them for opposing wolves, Fischer sought common ground. "The public has decided it wants wolves restored," Fischer explained, "so you can choose adamant opposition or cooperation. If you say 'hell, no! ' to wolves, you put yourself outside the process and will have no voice. If you cooperate, you become one of the players."

The Arizona Cattle Growers and the Arizona Wool Producers adopted resolutions favoring wolf reintroduction. The resolutions were highly conditional, but they were remarkable and unprecedented. Never before had the livestock industry shown even lukewarm tolerance for wolves, let alone official support for wolf recovery.

It is surprisingly difficult to turn public support for wolves into actual wolf feet on the ground. In New Mexico, a 1998 survey showed 79 percent of all state residents wanted wolves restored. But ranchers are more vehement about their position than are average citizens. By design, the American political system makes it difficult for a tepid majority to take actions opposed by a determined minority, especially a minority with good political connections.

A lawsuit by wolf advocates finally forced action. In 1993 FWS agreed to release wolves into New Mexico and Arizona. Finally, in 1996 the FWS completed an environmental impact statement. Although New Mexico had the most suitable wolf habitat, political opposition there caused FWS to turn its attention to Arizona, the only state willing to cooperate with the lobo restoration program.

The goal of the recovery program would be modest: to achieve a wild population of at least 100 lobos over 5,000 square miles of its historic range. The wild lobos would be backed up with a captive population of 200 animals held at approximately 30 different breeding sites. FWS might reconsider White Sands as a possible site, but the first effort would take place in the Apache National Forest of eastern Arizona.

As in the red wolf program, the first generation of zoo-bred animals were not expected to survive well. But if any of them had pups, those pups would be wild enough to do much better. And any pups they had would be wild lobos, the true goal of the program.

TRAGIC BEGINNINGS

To help the wolves make the transition from zoo animal to wild wolf, all wolves spent several months in "pre-acclimation pens." This was a new management technique added to the basic soft-release protocol used in the red wolf and Yellowstone releases.

Some extra measure was needed. The wolves released in Yellowstone had once been wild, and hunting was banned in the park. The red wolves released in the Alligator River National Wildlife Area were protected from humans by dense, swampy cover. Everything was against the lobo: tameness, the wide open Southwestern terrain, and all those pickups with rifles in their window gun racks. The lobo release would be the riskiest yet attempted in wolf restoration, hence managers gave the wolves the experience of pre-acclimation pens.

These confinement pens—sometimes called "wolf halfway houses"— are meant to allow wolves to become

Because of heavy development, wolf restoration in the Southwest will be more of a demonstration project than a general phenomenon. But it is no less important.

a little wilder than they had been in zoos. In zoos, wolves are fed by humans, which creates a sense of trust. In the pre-acclimation pens, wolves are given minimal contact with humans, and that contact is not pleasant. In some cases, live prey is introduced to the pens so the wolves can learn to kill it.

The zoo-born wolves spent about a year in these isolated pens before being moved to smaller confinement pens located in the actual release area. The wolves spent about a month in confinement pens in family groups, acquiring a sense of affinity to the area, after which the gates were opened.

The 11 wolves released on March 29, 1998, seemed to mark the successful end of a long, sad story. The Campbell Blue pack was an adult pair and two yearlings. The Hawk's Nest pack was an adult pair and two two-year offspring. The Turkey Creek group was a pair. Hopes were high.

On the whole, the "knuckleheads" didn't do badly. They learned to hunt cooperatively and kill elk. Although surrounded by cattle operations, they showed no inclination to attack cattle. One pair produced a pup, the first wild-born wolf in the Southwest in two decades. The wolves quickly learned to navigate in their new home areas.

The Campbell Blue pair produced the pup. When the female was shot, the male took over and tried to raise the pup. But the pup went missing, presumably dead. The male then began acting strangely, hanging around people and cattle for the first time. But he never attacked, and was eventually recaptured so he could be given a new mate and a fresh chance at life in the wild. He had done well. With a less tragic family history, he might have been entirely successful at the perilous transition from knucklehead to wild wolf.

Others weren't so successful. One female, wolf #494, took to digging trash near a restaurant in Alpine, Arizona. Some townsfolk were terrified to find a wolf in the city limits, but this wolf was anything but vicious. Her only depredation was an attack on a chicken coop that netted three chicks and a duck. Wolf #494 also suffered the ignominy of getting beaten up by a mule while a crowd of Memorial Day tourists watched in bug-eyed wonder. She was recaptured and returned to zoo life.

FIVE WOLVES

The first shooting triggered a controversy about law enforcement. A camper, Richard Humphrey, set up camp at an unauthorized site in the terrritory of the Turkey Creek pair. These wolves had already shown a tendency to hang around dogs. A wolf apparently got into a fight with one of Humphrey's dogs. Humphrey shot the male wolf, claiming he felt it was a threat to his family. Under questioning, Humphrey changed his story, and forensic evidence suggested both stories were probably fabricated. FWS officials decided not to prosecute him, perhaps hoping to avoid making a martyr of a man who could be seen as defending his family.

That decision became more controversial when the next four wolves were shot. Some wolf advocates believe the FWS decision to not prosecute Humphrey sent a message that wolf shootings would not be taken seriously. Other observers believe it was a messy case and that pursuing it aggressively could have inflamed public opinion against the young restoration program.

Managers had considered several factors when selecting the release site, and they had been obliged to make many compromises. Politics ultimately forced managers to release wolves in a region liberally laced with roads, open to public hunting, and close to the town of Alpine. Five dead wolves later, that decision looked less and less wise.

TRY, TRY AGAIN

Managers learned lessons with the first release that might help with subsequent releases. Above all, the second release will involve acclimation pens located farther from Alpine.

In the first release, acclimation pens might have been placed too close together. The Hawk's Nest group fought with the Campbell Blue pair because both groups ended up defending the same block of territory.

Managers have the option of tinkering with some details of future releases. This next year, some pups will be born in pre-acclimation pens rather than zoos, and that might make them just wild enough to make it. Releases might be timed to take place at different times of the year. The goal is to have wolves feeling comfortable in their ranges when elk begin producing calves.

But tinkering won't cure the basic problem. Tame wolves are being released in highly exposed country that is heavily used by humans, and not all of those humans will tolerate a coyote or a wolf.

Not long after the last of the first wolves were rounded up and returned to cages, two pairs of Mexican wolves were released into the wild again. Their thighs dotted with bright fluorescent paint, these "rainbow wolves" didn't look much like coyotes. Nearly a dozen more wolves were in acclimation pens, bonding with their areas and awaiting the day the pens would be opened. Other wolves might be transported by helicopter directly into the heart of the primitive area and hard-released into the wild. In all, FWS has plans to release as many as 17 more wolves back into the wild.

The message is clear: the FWS is serious about restoring lobos to the Southwest. In spite of the tragic beginning, the program will continue.

CHAPTER 11

The Truce in Alaska's Wolf War

Alaska is a big land, with a fifth as much land mass as all the Lower 48 states combined. Alaska is also home to more wolves than any other state, with a population estimated between 7,000 and 10,000 animals. The vast majority of those Alaskan wolves are *Canis lupus occidentalis*, the Mackenzie gray wolf, the largest race of wolves in the world. Pack sizes in Alaska run larger, too. While a typical pack has a dozen animals, researchers have documented packs with 30 wolves.

A decade ago, this big and beautiful land was the center of a rancorous wolf management debate. Newspapers ran stories with alarming headlines about proposed wolf "massacres." It seemed whenever state managers would propose some new wolf management program it would be challenged by lawsuits from wolf groups. Unhappiness with Alaska's

wolf management eventually led some environmental and wolf groups to declare a boycott of Alaska tourism.

Things are different now. The boycott has been canceled. The wrangling has subsided. The blizzard of lawsuits has dwindled to a few stray snowflakes. Alaska's wolf managers are no longer making news as they once did, although wolf groups continue to criticize some policies.

It would be nice to report that the reduced hostilities result from greater trust and understanding, but that might be overly optimistic. The spotlight of public attention that once was fixed on Alaska shifted southward when the fight to restore wolves to the Rockies reached its climax.

Other reasons for the change offer more hope for the future. A new governor decided the bad publicity Alaska was getting for its wolf pro-

Wolves are relatively abundant in Alaska, yet management controversies abound.

gram was costing the state too much good will. Governor Tony Knowles directed managers to halt lethal wolf control until a comprehensive review of wolf research could determine how scientifically valid it was. At the same time, the governor sought to create a new, open, participatory process for developing wolf management plans.

A DIFFERENT LAND

It's difficult for non-Alaskans to understand Alaska. Twice the size of Texas, the state contains fewer people than Rhode Island. The eastern south-central region has a few roads, but the vast interior is essentially roadless, accessible mainly by airplane.

Alaskans are different, too. Many moved to Alaska to get away from "civilization" and live closer to wildlife. Alaskans typically have a strong attachment to the natural world, but are less sentimental and more utilitarian in their wildlife values than citizens of the Lower 48. Alaskans generally love wolves, but some feel the state has more than it should.

Hunting is viewed differently in Alaska than in many regions of the United States. Citizens tend to see hunting as a natural, time-honored way of putting meat on the table.

Shooting a moose to be enjoyed on many dark winter evenings is more normal to many Alaskans than buying meat in plastic packages in stores with fluorescent lights.

ANTECEDENTS

Wolves were once persecuted as vigorously in Alaska as elsewhere, although they were never close to being extirpated. The state simply contains too much land, too many wolves, and too few people to drive wolf numbers that low.

Before the general availability of airplanes following World War II, wolves in Alaska were heavily trapped and snared. Then people learned how effectively they could kill wolves from airplanes. A 1955 *Field & Stream* article, entitled "Strafing Arctic Killers," described the practice. The author of the story congratulated himself for making more food available to Eskimo families by killing wolves. In the 1950s, federal authorities carried out a systematic anti-wolf program, using a combination of poison, traps, and gunners working from planes. A bounty encouraged private citizens to kill wolves.

Things changed in the 1960s, when state game agencies everywhere began hiring college graduates who had

majored in the new science of game management. The Alaska Department of Fish & Game (ADF&G) was formed when Alaska attained statehood in 1959. Although the department has been vilified for holding old-fashioned anti-wolf attitudes, it actually was born as one of the most pro-predator wildlife agencies in the nation, mostly because it was so new it didn't have a tradition of wolf eradication.

The prevailing theory at the time held that the "balance of nature" prevented predators from harming prey populations. The ADF&G dropped the wolf bounty and reduced wolf control programs shortly after statehood. Wolves were reclassified as big game animals, and wolf numbers began to increase.

Then, in the late 1960s and early 1970s, some specific moose and caribou populations plummeted to desperately low levels, triggering general alarm. The crisis initiated a debate

After World War II, Alaskans and visitors began hunting wolves from the air.

among Alaskans about what was wrong. Several factors were apparently responsible for the sharp decline in ungulate numbers. They included a succession of severe winters, an excessive harvest by human hunters, and heavy predation by wolves and bears.

The great concern about ungulate populations coincided with the appearance of research from northeastern Minnesota and elsewhere suggesting that wolves could suppress ungulate populations under some circumstances. Researchers argued that wolf predation was not as benign as they had formerly believed.

ADF&G managers limited moose and caribou hunting seasons and began reducing wolf numbers to let prey populations rebuild. The department also launched a series of research projects to study the complex web of predator-prey relationships. Several studies compared predator and prey populations in areas where wolves were controlled (by reducing their numbers) to those in areas where they were not controlled. In some

study areas, the department wanted to remove a large percentage of the wolves in order to determine whether ungulate populations would benefit.

WOLF WARS

That announcement alarmed environmental groups. Alaska appeared to be returning to the old, discredited practice of killing wolves just when the rest of the nation was learning to appreciate them. People in the Lower 48 were shocked to hear that hundreds of wolves—familiar to them as an "endangered species"—were being shot each year in Alaska. Critics either ignored the department's management objectives for experimenting with wolf control or they rejected those objectives as illegitimate.

Increasingly, disputes were resolved through lawsuits. Environmental groups began taking the ADF&G to court again and again. As the legal wars wore on, each side became increasingly impatient with the other. Many Alaskans began to feel under siege from arrogant and uninformed outsiders who wanted to turn Alaska into "one big park." Environmental groups dismissed Alaskans as anachronistic wolf-haters with no ecological sensitivity.

An early misunderstanding dealt with wolf numbers. The ADF&G had loosely estimated a wolf population of about 10,000 animals. In view of all the critical interest in wolves, the department conducted a more comprehensive count in 1984. When it produced a figure of 6,000 wolves, critics claimed Alaska's wolves had gone from 10,000 to 6,000 in just ten years, a frightening decline that seemed to justify their conviction that the state was persecuting its wolves. The department argued it could not be held responsible for the gap between an educated guess and the number produced by more careful science.

Most scientists today accept the department's claims that the state's population today stands somewhere between 7,000 and 10,000 wolves in about 800 packs. That overall figure has been holding steady for several years, although local populations rise and fall for various reasons. Wolf fans are concerned about losses suffered by one particular pack that has lived in Denali National Park. The Toklat pack has hunted outside Denali, where it has been depleted by trapping.

The annual hunting and trapping take for the whole state of Alaska is about 1,000 wolves, a number easily

Alaska's wolf population, with one notable exception, is doing fine.

sustained by a wolf population this big and well established. With one notable exception to be mentioned later, Alaska's wolves are doing well.

LAND-AND-SHOOT

A separate and equally contentious debate raged over "land-and-shoot" aerial hunting. The 1972 federal Airborne Hunting Act made it illegal to haze, herd, drive, harass, or shoot animals from airplanes. But it was still legal to spot a wolf or pack of wolves from the air, land a plane nearby, jump out, and shoot a wolf.

But the practice became increasingly controversial. Critics believed land-and-shoot hunters routinely broke the rules by shooting wolves from the air or hazing them to exhaustion before landing to finish them off. Since aerial hunting took place in remote country with no witnesses, meaningful enforcement of the restrictions was almost impossible. The image of hunting wolves from the air disgusted many people, including hunters who felt it violated the principle of "fair chase" and simply looked boorish.

In spite of negative publicity, the ADF&G continued to defend land-and-shoot wolf hunting. The department might have stuck with

land-and-shoot so stubbornly because eliminating the use of airplanes would limit its ability to run any kind of effective hunting season. In a large state with virtually no roads, it is extremely difficult to hunt wolves without using airplanes.

The land-and-shoot controversy gave the ADF&G a black eye by making the department appear insensitive to ethical and aesthetic values. Environmentalists seized on this issue as proof that the department was not to be trusted on any issue.

The controversy was settled with a 1996 ballot initiative. By a 57 to 43 percent margin, Alaskans decided to ban land-and-shoot hunting for several wildlife species, including wolves.

WOLF CONTROL
AND UNGULATES

A primary responsibility of the ADF&G is to maintain ungulate populations—principally moose and caribou—at acceptable levels. The state's charter mandates that the department do this for the benefit of all Alaskans.

Moreover, a major source of income in Alaska is the money brought to the state by hunters from the Lower 48. Each nonresident moose hunter who visits Alaska

leaves several thousand dollars in the state's economy. That money is appreciated in Alaska, as it would be in any other state. Since many industries, such as farming and manufacturing, are incompatible with Alaska's geography and remote location, the state has traditionally seen its natural resources as a legitimate source of income.

Critics of the ADF&G's wolf programs charged that the department was selling out to the interests of the guided hunt industry. Wolves would die, they argued, just so wealthy hunters could have more targets.

Dick Bishop is a retired biologist active in Alaskan conservation causes. "I've attended umpty-ump resource meetings all over the state," Bishop says. "They showed me that the economic motive is not uppermost in the minds of most Alaskans. What matters to Alaskans is the opportunity to hunt for their own meat. People have strong feelings

Surveys indicate that Alaskans have great affection for wolves.

Recent changes in Alaska's approach to wolf management have sharply reduced legal and political conflicts.

about that."

Research done in Alaska and elsewhere convinced ADF&G managers that ungulate populations that fall to low levels for whatever reasons—often bad weather—can be artificially held down by predators. The phrase coined for this was having ungulates trapped in "a predator pit." Research argued that Alaska had a special problem with multiple predators, principally bears and wolves. When moose and caribou numbers dropped to low levels, the combination of grizzly bear, black bear, and wolf predation in spring would destroy so many recently born ungulates that the local moose and caribou herds would be pinned at levels far lower than the environment would otherwise permit.

A number of studies in Alaska and the Yukon documented the dangers of heavy predation on young ungulates. If predators kill over 90 percent of the caribou calves—as they did in some studies—caribou numbers are pinned at low levels. Moose are even more vulnerable. Typically, 100 cow moose give birth to about 120 to 140 calves each year. In some studies, predators whittled that group to just 10 to 20 survivors at summer's end. Moose cannot sustain population levels while losing 90 percent of their young each year.

The issue is complex, and the research does not point in one direction. Caribou seem better able than moose to rebound from population lows, apparently because they migrate. Still, the weight of research from Alaska and the Yukon suggests that heavy predation on young ungulates can prevent a distressed population from rebuilding to the level the habitat should be able to sustain. Wolf control seemed the best answer to restoring ungulate numbers.

Frankly, there aren't many manipulations available to Alaska's managers that might increase moose or caribou numbers. Habitat alterations would be expensive and difficult in the roadless terrain. Moreover, habitat didn't seem to be the problem in many cases, since ungulates were holding at much lower levels than the habitat in certain regions had historically supported. Since predation seemed to be the factor holding ungulate numbers at low levels, predator control seemed the best answer.

Why concentrate predator control on wolves when bears are a major part of the problem? Bears are long-lived species with relatively low fertility. If managers were to goof and allow too many bears to be killed in an area, the mistake might be difficult to remedy. Wolves, with their great fertility, can take heavy losses and bounce back quickly, so it seems more prudent to aim control measures at wolves.

Why not limit the take by humans? ADF&G research showed predators took as much as five times the number of ungulates that hunters did. Limiting the predation by humans wouldn't make much of a difference, although it could be part of a more comprehensive solution.

Managers even experimented with "diversionary feeding" of predators in the spring when freshly calved ungulates are most vulnerable. This involved flying road-killed moose or other animals into regions where wolves were a problem. Presumably, the presence of road-killed meat would reduce predation on newborn ungulates. Unfortunately, the program was as expensive as expected without being as effective as hoped.

THE BALANCE OF NATURE

A common objection raised by wolf fans is that wolves and ungulates should be left alone so the "balance of nature" can set their population levels. ADF&G managers had several answers based on research, but wolf fans familiar with early research on wolf-prey systems were suspicious of research done in Alaska and elsewhere that complicated the picture of how wolves and their prey interrelate.

Alaska wildlife managers pointed out that Alaska is unusual because it has multiple predators preying on ungulates. Studies done on Isle Royale involve only moose and wolves, and even that radically simplified predator-prey system turns out to be more complex than researchers once thought. Alaska managers claim it is dangerous for a baby caribou or moose to be born into a world full of black bears, grizzly bears, *and* wolves.

Then there is the issue of what sort of balance of nature is desirable. Recent research suggests predator-prey systems rarely exhibit a static balance, but swing back and forth constantly in response to such factors as weather events, parasite infestations, changes in the forest succession, and so forth. Alaska's managers argue that it is foolishly passive to wait for a predator-prey system to slowly return to health when a little artful fiddling could bring about healthy animal populations much more quickly.

For many years, a prevailing conviction among Alaska's wildlife managers has been that wolf-bear-ungulate pop-

ulations can be more or less stable at different levels of abundance. Research suggested the "normal" condition with no human manipulation would yield a stable system with very few ungulates and very few predators. That did not seem terribly desirable. By temporarily depressing wolf numbers, managers believed they could create a new dynamic balance with both ungulates and predators existing at much higher levels.

That "win-win" condition seemed so desirable it justified wolf control. All managers had to do was eliminate enough wolves for enough years so that the moose and caribou could scramble out of the predator pit. Then everyone—wolf fans, Native Alaskans, white Alaskans, and sport hunters from the Lower 48—could enjoy an Alaska blessed with a new abundance of moose, caribou, bears, *and* wolves.

Unfortunately, wolf control isn't pretty and it isn't easy. To significantly reduce wolf numbers, it is necessary to kill a *lot* of wolves. Wolf packs can lose 30 to 40 percent of their adult members every year without dwindling. Losses among the adults leads to greater production and survival among the pups. To reduce wolf numbers it is necessary to kill more than

An experiment in nonlethal wolf control to help the weakened Fortymile caribou herd seems to be working.

half of the adults and do it year after year. No matter what the rationale might be, killing that many wolves was bound to be controversial. Critics questioned the research, doubted the motives of Alaska managers, and protested that killing so many wolves for *any* purpose was wrong.

NEW APPROACHES

The chronic conflict over Alaska's wolf management was extracting such a price on the state's reputation that Governor Tony Knowles determined to create a new climate for developing and discussing wolf policies.

One of Knowles' first measures was to call for a neutral scientific review of Alaska's research on predators and ungulates. In 1994, Knowles suspended predator control measures until the scientific rationale for them had been carefully considered. A special committee of the National Research Council, a part of the National Academy of Sciences, was formed to analyze the research on predators and ungulates.

The committee's report, published in 1997, disappointed partisans on both sides of the issue by being equivocal. Essentially, the committee found that predator-ungulate interrelationships are complex to study and difficult to manipulate. The group praised the ADF&G for its extensive research, which is perhaps the best in the country, then went on to say that those studies were not sufficient to make a compelling case for lethal predator control. The council's economic analysis suggested it would become difficult to justify wolf control on a cost-benefit ratio basis, given the increasing cost of wolf control and increasingly negative public attitudes about lethal wolf control. The report made a number of specific recommendations and concluded, predictably, with a call for more and better studies.

The most remarkable wolf management initiative of the Knowles administration was a dramatically new program designed to restore the famous Fortymile caribou herd. This management protocol was developed by a planning team representing the many "stakeholders" with an interest in the caribou. Hunters, environmentalists, and others met to agree on management objectives and then hammer out a plan that might achieve them. All groups participating in the process ended up making significant concessions.

The Fortymile caribou herd has fallen to five percent of its former size, using only a fourth of its former range. Hard winters, predation, and overharvesting are thought to have caused the collapse of this herd. Researchers believed that without predator control, this herd might not restore its numbers for as long as 50 to 100 years.

The plan developed by the consensus planning team featured what is probably the first major experiment with nonlethal wolf control. Wolf packs suspected of pinning caribou numbers down are being thinned by sterilizing the alpha pair and translocating other pack members. The translocation process mimics the natural process of dispersal. To sterilize the alphas, veterinarians perform the same operation used to sterilize pet dogs. The rationale for sterilizing the alphas and leaving them in place is that they will probably defend their territory against other wolves. Hunters are also reducing their take of caribou.

Many questions remain to be answered about this expensive and innovative experiment, but early results are encouraging. Although sterilization and translocation have been applied to only five of 15 wolf packs in the area, the caribou herd is up 20 percent already and seems poised to rebound quickly. Even this "nonlethal" control has critics among wolf fans, as some think translocating wolves is dangerous. Obviously, this experiment will require a great deal of close study to evaluate long-range impacts on all the animals involved.

ALEXANDER ARCHIPELAGO WOLF

A possibly distinctive wolf lives in southeast Alaska, principally on the many large and small islands that comprise the Tongass National Forest. The Alexander Archipelago wolf, *Canis lupus ligoni*, was once considered a separate gray wolf subtype but now is thought by some taxonomists to be a geographically isolated group of the Great Plains wolf that is common in so much of Canada and the United States. Researchers aren't sure how distinct it is.

This issue is important. If it is just another *nubilis* wolf, the Alexander Archipelago wolf is not endangered except in this very specific region. If it is a distinctive gray wolf subtype, it is highly endangered indeed because the population stands somewhere near 1,000 individuals and the long-range trends are unfavorable.

This wolf primarily feeds upon Sitka deer, a small race of black-tailed deer related to mule deer. These wolves also prey upon beavers, fish, and birds, but the keystone prey species is the Sitka deer. As it goes, so goes the Alexander Archipelago wolf. And the Sitka deer faces a bleak future unless logging practices in the Tongass are changed significantly.

Sitka deer have evolved to live in the coastal old-growth forests. But clear-cut logging is eroding that habitat base. Right after the loggers leave an area, deer and wolves thrive for about 20 years because the first plants to appear offer food and shelter. But when second-growth trees grow tall enough to shut out almost all of the sunlight from the forest floor, the forage needed by the deer disappears. Present logging practices create immediate gains but long-term losses for deer and wolves.

It is possible to log the Tongass Forest in ways that favor Sitka deer and wolves, but those logging protocols would be so expensive that they will probably face enormous resistance from the U.S. Forest Service. Loggers would have to remove trees very selectively rather than clear-cutting a large area at once. Given the rugged terrain of this region, that approach would have little appeal to an agency increasingly asked to defend itself economically. Cessation of logging is not an option. Both in local communities and among the Alaska congressional delegation, there is very strong sentiment in favor of continued logging in the Tongass Forest.

Less costly measures might help a little. Managers might leave a series of "forest reserves" where species that do well in old-growth forests would presumably have a chance to live. But that would leave wolves a small amount of fragmented habitat. Hunting and trapping seasons could be adjusted to protect wolves. Wolf mortality is high near old logging roads, but it seems politically impossible to close a road once it has been created, so that inexpensive option seems precluded by public opinion.

A recent study concluded that "without significant changes to the Tongass Land Management Plan, the long-term viability of the Alexander Archipelago wolf is seriously imperiled." Anyone familiar with the workings of federal agencies might predict that researchers will be under pressure to decide this wolf isn't unique after all. Or, perhaps more likely, wildlife mangers will be pressured to agree that some relatively inexpensive programs will give it sufficient protection. The Alexander Archipelago wolf is standing in the path of a speeding logging truck, and it isn't likely the truck is going to swerve just to miss the wolf.

The wolves of Alaska, appropriately for this big land, are the largest race of gray wolf known.

CHAPTER 12

What Is the Future for Wolves?

Recent events have proven how difficult it is to make predictions about the future of wolf restoration.

For example, nobody could have predicted how long and divisive the Yellowstone controversy would be. It has long been evident that the public overwhelmingly wants wolves in Yellowstone and that there is probably no place on earth that is better suited to host wolves.

But inevitably, irrelevant external issues got mixed in with the wolf restoration issue, until the Yellowstone reintroduction became a showdown in the fight over who would control the future of the West. In the end, wolves were returned to the park, but only after two decades of bitter battles. Nobody could have predicted a wildlife management decision would incite so much passion.

And now the Yellowstone controversy has taken another turn nobody could have foreseen. Who could have foreseen that a judge would rule against a singular achievement of the Endangered Species Act (ESA) because—*of all things*—it violates the ESA?

Similarly, nobody would have predicted that the first release of wolves in the Southwest would result in five gun-shot wolves. Managers knew the release site was compromised, but five dead wolves was an outcome worse than the worst-case scenario in anyone's mind when managers opened the doors of the acclimation pens.

At the same time, few observers could have predicted wolf restoration would proceed as smoothly as it has in the Western Great Lakes states. Michigan and Wisconsin are in a honeymoon period of expanding wolf populations with almost no conflicts between wolves and people. With plenty of deer to prey on and few

The wolf's prospects are brighter now than they were a decade ago, but the battle for wolf restoration has not been won.

farms to tempt them, the wolves of Wisconsin and Michigan have been model citizens. Many people are genuinely thrilled that the howl of the wolf is heard again in their region.

Who would have predicted such broad acceptance of wolves in states that just decades ago had bounties on wolves in order to get rid of them?

MINNESOTA

The most important state to watch

to see how wolves and people are going to get along is my home state of Minnesota because nowhere else are so many wolves living near so many people. Wolves, having occupied the areas once thought to be the only good wolf habitat in the state, are now dispersing into developed regions where wolves have not been seen in the twentieth century. Wolves are living virtually on the outskirts of the Twin Cities metropolitan region

A manager tranquilizes a timber wolf in Northern Wisconsin.

and may show up in the suburbs soon. A news report I heard while writing this paragraph said wolves were a "traffic hazard" on the roads around one small northern town. Four wolves were killed by cars there in recent days.

In effect, wolves have forced a re-definition of "wolf habitat." Managers used to think wolves needed wilderness areas to survive. They conducted research that tried to define just how wild—how roadless and free of human use—a region had to be in order to function as wolf habitat. Forget all that. Wolf experts now define wolf habitat as "anywhere there is enough food and enough human toleration."

The first decades of the new millennium will be a fascinating test of the limits of human tolerance. For the first time in the modern era, great numbers of humans and many wolves are occupying the same territory. So far there is no great groundswell of opinion demanding that wolf numbers be seriously reduced. Minnesotans argue about how many wolves the state should have, but in the context of the horrific wolf wars elsewhere in the country, this is a family squabble, not a real wolf fight.

The great fight to win public acceptance of wolves is largely over in the Western Great Lakes. The wolves won. The smattering of wolf hatred coming from unsuccessful deer hunters, some livestock spokesmen, and a handful of barstool wildlife wizards does not amount to serious opposition to wolves. Illegal wolf killings take place, but not at a level that prevents wolves from expanding numbers and range. Meanwhile, environmental and wolf groups have lined up solidly to make sure the wolf never again drifts anywhere near "endangered" status in this region again.

Alas, that does not ensure a solid future for the wolf in Minnesota and the other Great Lakes states. I trust wolves will do well in the short term, perhaps the next 30 or 40 years, but I brood about two long-range trends.

First is the continued loss of habitat. Many regions where I hunted grouse a few years ago are filling up with cabins and homes. To its shame, Minnesota hasn't begun to deal with urban sprawl. Bit by bit, acre by acre, deep woods are becoming woodsy suburbs. That's not good for wolves, even if human toleration has expanded the notion of what wolf habitat can be. If the whole state becomes one big suburb, where will wolves live?

My second concern is long-range but spooky. Scientists no longer debate whether the greenhouse effect will change our world. The issue now is how soon the changes will come and how destabilizing they will be. Previous climatic changes have led to changes in forest species composition, but those previous climate changes were so gradual that forest types could evolve naturally in response. The abrupt climate changes forced by the greenhouse effect might alter our northern forests so radically that forests will die instead of evolving.

When that happens, the future of the wolf will be a trivial issue, relatively speaking. We might someday look back on the old wolf restoration wars with nostalgia because they took place in such an innocent, easy time.

THE WEST

The future of wolves in the West and Southwest is almost surely better than the recent past would indicate.

Wolves will continue to do well in the Northern Rockies if the Downes decision is reversed, as it almost surely will be. Yellowstone and central Idaho are superb wolf habitat. Wolves have not shown a preference for fat cattle over lean elk, defying the predictions of many fearful ranchers. Wolves in the Rockies also got lucky when Ed Bangs was named to head up the federal wolf restoration program. Bangs has a remarkable ability to minimize conflict. He is the ideal person to show ranchers that wolves are in the West to stay, but that that will not spell the end of the world as they have known it.

There will be problems. Wolves will occasionally attack livestock, and they will have to be dealt with promptly. Western livestock producers might need to improve their animal husbandry practices to prevent depredation, and sometimes that will add to the expense of doing business. Elk hunting outfitters might sometimes be affected by the presence of a new predator. Where wolves create real problems, managers should seek real solutions that respect the interests of all. Some wolf fans need to improve their understanding of the problems wolves can cause for people who live near them.

Alas, the Southwest is too highly developed to permit the same kind of extensive comeback being seen in the Northern Rockies. The return of the lobo will be more of a demonstration project than a broad-scale return as it is in Yellowstone and Idaho. Yet the lobo is terribly important—genetically, historically, and culturally—and its return to at least some wild regions of

The renewal of the ESA is critical, but nothing is more important to the wolf's future than public education.

the Southwest is highly desirable. If the state of New Mexico ever learns to accept wolves, the program is much more likely to succeed.

After talking to many people in the Southwest, I am cautiously optimistic about the Mexican wolf. The tragic beginning of the restoration program is likely to remain a mystery, but I cannot believe it forecasts the future of the program as well. Too many people in the Southwest want wolves out there somewhere. It will happen.

EDUCATION

Sound wolf management depends upon sound, factual information. That used to mean that people needed to learn that wolves aren't the threat they have been portrayed to be. Because some wolf groups have deified and romanticized the wolf, today it is sometimes as necessary to correct the myths of wolf advocates as the distortions of wolf haters. Wolf managers who used to suffer abuse from wolf haters increasingly find

themselves under assault from groups that cannot distinguish between legitimate wolf management and wolf persecution.

One thing badly needed is a new technology for limiting wolf numbers without killing wolves. Wildlife management has not developed many tools for controlling the numbers of population. The main technique is to have a hunting season to lower a certain animal population. But it is increasingly difficult for managers to convince the public it is necessary to kill wolves. It is hard to say whether Alaska's recent experiment with wolf neutering points the way to wolf management in the future.

Many nonprofit organizations now work to help wolves. A highly select few include the following.

The International Wolf Center (IWC) in Ely, Minnesota, is probably the wolf education center most respected by wolf scientists around the world. The IWC conducts a number of programs designed to promote accurate understanding of wolves, including educational field trips. The attractive center houses the original

To make good management decisions, people need to shove aside prejudice and confront verifiable fact, which isn't often done.

"Of Wolves and Men" exhibit and has a pack of ambassador wolves. Sometimes criticized by more strident groups for not being confrontational in wolf wars, the IWC works hard to represent the accumulated knowledge of the world's eminent wolf researchers and managers. The IWC is committed to defending the future of wolves by presenting accurate, reliable, balanced information. It has an award-winning Internet site at http://www.wolf.org.

The Wolf Recovery Foundation (WRF) works for wolf restoration in the northern Rockies. This respected organization promotes better understanding of wolves through a variety of programs, conferences, and workshops. The WRF is researching the use of burros as guard animals to protect livestock from wolves. Located in Idaho, the WRF is an effective partner in the long effort to return wolves to the northern Rockies.

The Julian Wolf Preserve, in San Diego County, wants to promote a better understanding of wildlife by concentrating on the plight of the gray wolf. The Wolf Preserve has a high commitment to education and research, exhibiting gray wolves in a natural pack setting and presenting educational programs each week to the public. The Preserve participates in the Mexican wolf recovery program and is one of the centers raising these highly endangered gray wolves for release into the wild.

The Wildlife Science Center, a relative newcomer to the world of nonprofit wolf education centers, is located just north of the Twin Cities in Minnesota. This center promotes understanding of wolves through a variety of educational programs, including summertime "Bonfire Wolf Howls." Several dozen wolves are maintained, including red wolves and some wolves with intriguing personal histories. The staff of the center is ardent about wolves but realistic about the occasional need for management to minimize wolf-human conflicts. The center does a great deal of research with wolf immobilization techniques that are used by restoration biologists all over the country.

Alaska, the state with the most wolves of all, is well served by Wolf Song of Alaska. The group's Internet site is an excellent source of accurate, balanced information. The address is http://www.wolfsongalaska.org. The group is working on a major observation facility to be located in Anchorage. When finished, it will be a state-of-the-art wolf education and information center.

The National Wildlife Federation (NWF) led the fight to secure Endangered Species Act protection for wolves and, along with its independent state affiliates, has played a long and important role in wolf restoration efforts nationwide. NWF wolf recovery team members have worked with public and private agencies to tailor common-sense management plans and to secure wolf recovery. At the same time, the National Wildlife Federation has developed public education programs focused on the facts and myths surrounding the animal. With new federal plans to enhance species management about to be announced, NWF continues to ensure that the Endangered Species Act keeps its promise.

Defenders of Wildlife (DOW) has long worked for wolf restoration. Above all, it was DOW's innovative depredation compensation program that played a critical role in returning wolves to the Northern Rockies. That same fund is now helping make a place for the lobo in the Southwest. Unlike the groups mentioned so far, DOW also maintains an aggressive legal office that attempts to help wolves in the courts, where so much wildlife management policy is determined.

Internet web sites are so ephemeral that listing them in a book is often fruitless, yet two others deserve mention. Ralph Maughan is an informed, passionate, and industrious student of wildlife management controversies. He maintains a bulky, slow-loading but fascinating web site that, among other things, tracks the comings and goings of individual wolves in the Rockies. The current address for Ralph Maughan's Report is http://www.poky.srv.net~jjmrm/.

The Wolf Justice League has a site with an exceptionally lively and informative "Outpost" forum discussion. Anyone can find these sites by typing the names into a search engine. The Wolf Justice League's home page address is http://spiritwolf.reliacom/wjl/.

THE SECOND CHANCE

While my work on this book has convinced me that it is foolish to reduce wolves to symbols, I believe the restoration of wolves will be one of the major symbolic events in human history. Humans in general—and Americans in particular—have abused wolves. We owe it to the wolf to try one more time to work out a relationship that protects legitimate human interests while allowing living

When our society has learned to live with wolves, we can begin to like ourselves a little better.

space for wolves.

Further, I would argue, we owe it to ourselves to try again to manage wolves wisely. When Americans learn to tolerate and respect wolves, we will have exorcised something singularly ugly in our national character.

While I believe wolf restoration is going to proceed successfully in many regions, I don't expect it to be easy. Greed, fear, and other deep-seated human traits will continue to complicate our relationship with wolves.

Moreover, the wolves themselves will keep the process edgy. Wolves aren't saints. Wolves are smart, strong, and resourceful. When they begin attacking livestock, they can be formidable opponents. As wolves increasingly live near people, they are likely to attack beloved pets. Wolves reproduce quickly and move around rapidly. Unless they are in a wilderness setting, wolves can be a tricky animal to manage.

A crucial issue for the future is whether or not humans and wolves can live together if humans do nothing to keep wolves afraid of us. When people stop being a threat to wolves, wolves are smart enough to recognize

that fact. The fear of humans is not in their genes but in their heads, based on centuries of persecution. Take away the persecution and you take away the fear of humans. The resulting animal might be more of a threat to humans than wolf fans now choose to believe.

It may be part of the long, tragic history of humans and wolves that the price of living with wolves may be continued human aggression against wolves. This is not a position I enjoy adopting. Obviously, we do not need to persecute wolves as we have historically. But it seems likely that we will need to harass or even hunt them enough to keep them wary of us, perhaps by having a carefully controlled hunting season. I am open to the possibility that wolves and humans might be able to live "in peace" with each other, but my better judgment tells me it is necessary for humans to exhibit enough measured aggression toward wolves to keep them wary of us.

The true measure of the morality of a political society is how justly it treats its least powerful and popular citizens. In much the same sense, the ecological decency of a society can be measured by how it treats the most troublesome and notorious animal species. For our society, that is the wolf.

When our society proves it has learned to live with wolves, we can begin to like ourselves a little better. It will then be time to ponder how we can improve our relations with several hundred other species, but not before pausing to celebrate the extraordinary progress represented by the return of the wolf.

INDEX